RISC-V
Assembly Language

```
rv Version 3.4                        Mon Jul 15 02:25:45 2019
Anthony J. Dos Reis

Header
R
L 00000000
L 00000004
C


Loc     Code            Source Code
0000    0141a283            lw t0, x        # load 2 into t0
0004    0181a303            lw t1, y        # load 3 into t1
0008    006282b3            add t0, t0, t1  # add t0 and t1
000c    04028000            dout t0         # display sum in t0
0010    00000000            halt            # terminate program
0014    00000002 x:         .word 2         # data (2)
0018    00000003 y:         .word 3         # data(3)
==================================================== Output
5
================================================ Program statistics
Input file name       = r0301.a
Instructions executed = 5 (decimal)
Program size          = 1c (hex) 28 (decimal)
Load point            = 0 (hex) 0 (decimal)
Programmer            = Anthony J. Dos Reis
```

Anthony J. Dos Reis

RISC-V Assembly Language edition 1
Copyright © 2019 by Anthony J. Dos Reis, all rights reserved

ISBN: 9781088462003

1 0 9 8 7 6 5 4 3 2

Preface

This book presents RISC-V assembly language with emphasis on system concepts. You will learn not only assembly language programming but also the system concepts necessary to fully understand the machine level of a RISC-V computer that supports the RV32I and RV32M instruction sets. The only prerequisite for this book is familiarity with some programming language. The topics covered include

- Numbering systems
- RISC-V architecture
- Machine language
- Assembly language, assemblers, and the assembly process
- Multiplication and division in software and hardware
- Linkers and the linking process
- Compiling C code to RISC-V

The rv RISC-V assembler/linker/debugger/interpreter in the software package for this book provides the perfect programming environment in which to learn RISC-V assembly language and architecture. It has some significant advantages over the typical programming/debugging/testing environment:

- Runs on Windows, Mac OS X, Linux, and Raspbian.
- Simple installation: Unzip the distribution file into the directory of your choosing.
- Provides run-time error messages that pinpoint the location of the error—no cryptic "Segmentation error" or "Program has stopped working" messages. Detects and terminates infinite loops.
- Provides a simple-to-use but powerful symbolic debugger.
- Supports simple-to-use and system independent I/O instructions.
- Includes a linker.
- Accepts not only assembly language source code but text files containing machine language programs in binary or hex.
- Produces student-named, time-stamped assembly listings that include run-time output.

To get the latest version of the software package, send an email to rvtextbook@gmail.com. You will then immediately receive an automatic reply with a link to the site at which you can download the software package (rv.zip).

Anthony J. Dos Reis
SUNY New Paltz
dosreist@newpaltz.edu

Table of Contents

4 Assembly Language Part 2

5 Multiplication and Division

6 Linking

7 Compiling C Code to RISC-V

1 Numbering Systems

Decimal, Binary, and Hexadecimal

Decimal is a positional numbering system. It is so called because in a decimal number the contribution of each digit to the value of the number depends not only on the digit but on its position in the number. For example, consider the three-digit decimal number 123:

$$\frac{1 \quad 2 \quad 3}{100 \quad 10 \quad 1} \quad \text{weights}$$

Each position has a weight. In a whole number, weights start with 1 and increase from right to left by a factor of 10 from each position to the next. The value of the number is given by the sum of each digit times its weight. Thus, the value of 123 is

$$1 \times 100 + 2 \times 10 + 3 \times 1$$

The 1 digit contributes $1 \times 100 = 100$ to the value of the number; the 2 digit contributes $2 \times 10 = 20$ to the value of the number, the 3 digit contributes $3 \times 1 = 3$ to the value of the number. Although the 3 digit is greater than the 2 digit, the 2 digit contributes more to the value of the number than the 3 digit because its weight is ten times that of the 3 digit.

We call decimal the *base-10* numbering system because it uses 10 distinct symbols and because weights increase by a factor of 10 from each position to the next. *Binary* is the *base-2* numbering system. It uses two distinct symbols (0 and 1), called *bits*. In binary, position weights increase by a factor of 2 from each position to the next. For example, consider the five-bit binary number 01101:

$$\frac{0 \quad 1 \quad 1 \quad 0 \quad 1}{16 \quad 8 \quad 4 \quad 2 \quad 1} \quad \text{weights}$$

Its value is given by the sum of each digit times its weight:

$$0 \times 16 + 1 \times 8 + 1 \times 4 + 0 \times 2 + 1 \times 1 = 13 \text{ decimal}$$

It is easy to determine the decimal value of a binary number: Simply add up the weights corresponding to the 1 bits. In the binary number above, the weights corresponding to 1 bits are 8, 4, and 1. Thus, the value of the number is $8 + 4 + 1 = 13$ decimal.

We call a sequence of eight bits a *byte*. For example, 1111000010101010 consists of two bytes: 11110000 and 10101010. To *complement* a bit means to flip it. That is, change a 1 bit to 0, and a 0 bit to 1.

Hexadecimal (or hex for short) is the *base-16* numbering system. It uses 16 symbols: 0 to 9 and A, B, C, D, E, and F in upper or lower case (the lowercase forms are more convenient for keyboard input because their entry do not require the shift key). The values of A, B, C, D, E, and F and their corresponding lowercase forms equal decimal 10, 11, 12, 13, 14, and 15, respectively.

Weights in a hexadecimal number increase by a factor of 16. For example, consider the three-digit hex number 2C5:

$$\frac{2 \quad C \quad 5}{256 \quad 16 \quad 1} \text{ weights (in decimal)}$$

Its value is given by

$$2\times256 + C\times16 + 5\times1$$

The hex digit C is 12 in decimal so the expression above using only decimal is equal to

$$2\times256 + 12\times16 + 5\times1 = 512 + 192 + 5 = 709$$

The following table shows the decimal numbers from 0 to 15 and their binary and hex equivalents.

Decimal	Binary	Hex
0	0000	0
1	0001	1
2	0010	2
3	0011	3
4	0100	4
5	0101	5
6	0110	6
7	0111	7
8	1000	8
9	1001	9
10	1010	A (or a)
11	1011	B (or b)
12	1100	C (or c)
13	1101	D (or d)
14	1110	E (or e)
15	1111	F (or f)

Since we will be working quite a bit with binary and hex, *it is essential that you memorize this table.*

If you append a 0 on the right side of a binary whole number, the weight of each digit increases by a factor of 2. Thus, the value of the number doubles. For example, 3 in binary is 0011. If we append a 0, we get 0110, which is 6 decimal. If we append another 0, we get 1100, which is 12 decimal. Of course, adding a 0 on the left side does not affect the value of a number. For example, 0110 equals 00110.

Similarly, if you append a 0 on the right side of a hex whole number, its value increases by a factor of 16 (since the weight of each digit increases by a factor of 16). For example, A is 10 decimal, and A0 is 160 decimal.

Rule: Adding a 0 on the right side of a positional whole number multiplies its value by its base.

Numbering Bits

The bits in a binary number are numbered right to left starting with 0. For example, in an eight-bit number, the rightmost bit is bit 0; the leftmost bit is bit 7:

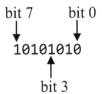

With this numbering scheme, there is a nice correspondence between a bit's number and its weight: Bit i has weight 2^i. For example, bit 3 in the binary number above has the weight $2^3 = 8$. Thus, it contributes 8 to the value of the number.

The leftmost bit and the rightmost bit in a binary number are called the *most significant bit* (abbreviated msb) and the *least significant bit* (abbreviated lsb), respectively.

Adding Positional Numbers

Let's quickly review how we add two decimal numbers. Consider the following addition:

```
    1   carries
  157
+ 238
  395
```

We start in the right column. Adding 7 and 8, we get 15. The result is two digits. So we record the right digit 5 at the bottom of the column and carry the left digit 1 to the next column. Thus, in the next column we add 1, 5, and 3 to get 9. The result is a single digit so we do not carry into the next column. Finally, we add 1 and 2 in the left column to get 3 for that column.

To add two binary numbers, we take exactly the same approach as we take with decimal. For example, consider the following addition of the binary numbers 0011 and 0011:

```
   11   carries
  0011
+ 0011
  0110
```

When we add the right column, we get 10 binary (2 decimal). The result is two bits. So we record the right bit 0 and carry the left bit 1 to the next column. Thus, in the next column, we add 1, 1, and 1 to get 11 binary (3 decimal). So we record the right bit 1 and carry the left bit 1 to the next column, where we add 1, 0, and 0 to get 1. Finally, in the leftmost column, we add 0 and 0 to get 0.

Let's now add the hex numbers 1B and 37:

```
  1   carries
  1B
+ 37
  52
```

Adding B (11 in decimal) and 7, we get 12 hex (18 decimal). We record the 2 digit and carry 1 to the next column, where we add 1, 1, and 3 to get 5.

Representing Negative Binary Numbers

Signed numbers within a computer are usually represented in the *two's complement* system. Before we discuss two's complement, let's make a simple observation. Suppose a computer represents numbers using only 4 bits. If our computer adds 0001 to 1111, what is the result? Here is the addition:

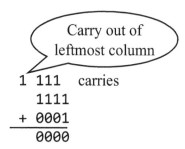

```
1 111   carries
  1111
+ 0001
  0000
```

We get zero with a carry out of the leftmost column. Since we are assuming the computer uses only four bits to represent numbers, this carry in not included in the result. Thus, the result is 0000.

Rule: Adding 1 to a binary number with a fixed number of bits all of which are 1 results in all zeros.

Let's now experimentally determine the two's complement representation of -3. We want the binary form of -3 that when added to the binary form of $+3$ gives a sum of zero. Let's see if complementing (i.e., flipping) all the bits in the binary form of $+3$ is the desired representation of -3:

```
  0011  = +3
+ 1100  = +3 with each bit flipped
  1111
```

We do not get zero so 1100 is not -3. But recall our preceding rule: Adding 1 to all 1's gives zero. Thus, because flipping the bits of $+3$ gives all 1's when added to $+3$, flipping the bits *and* adding 1 should give us the representation that produces zero when added to $+3$. Let's try it. Flipping the bits of $+3$ and adding 1, we get

```
  1100  = +3  with each bit flipped
+ 0001  add 1
  1101  Is this -3?
```

Is 1101 the representation of -3 that we want? Let's add it to $+3$ to see if it gives zero:

```
1 111   carries
  0011  = +3
+ 1101  Is this -3?
  0000
```

We, indeed, get zero with a carry out of the leftmost position. Thus, 1101 is the correct representation of -3 in the two's complement system.

Rule: To negate a binary number in the two's complement system, flip its bits and add 1.

The binary number system that can represent both positive and negative numbers and in which a number is negated by flipping its bits and adding 1 is called the *two's complement system*. We call the negation of a number the *two's complement* of that number. For example, the two's complement of 0011 (+3) is 1101 (−3). The two's complement of 1101 (−3) should get us back to is 0011 (+3). Indeed, it does:

$$
\begin{array}{r}
\texttt{0010} \quad = -3 \text{ with each bit flipped} \\
+ \quad\quad \texttt{1} \\
\hline
\texttt{0011} \quad = +3
\end{array}
$$

To add two's complement numbers, we simply add them using the standard adding procedure. It does not matter if one is positive and one is negative. For example, lets add +1 and −3. The result should be the two's complement number for −2:

$$
\begin{array}{r}
\texttt{0001} \quad = +1 \\
+ \ \texttt{1101} \quad = -3 \\
\hline
\texttt{1110} \quad = -2
\end{array}
$$

To confirm that 1110 is −2, take its two's complement to see if you get +2. That is, flip the bits in 1110 and add 1. The result is indeed 0010 (+2), which confirms that 1101 is −2.

In the two's complement system, −1 is represented with all 1's. Let's confirm this by taking the two's complement of +1. We flip the bits in +1 and add 1. We get

$$
\begin{array}{r}
\texttt{1110} \quad = +1 \text{ with each bit flipped} \\
+ \quad\quad \texttt{1} \\
\hline
\texttt{1111} \quad = -1
\end{array}
$$

Rule: In the two's complement system, all 1's represents −1.

In the two's complement system, the leftmost bit of a number indicates the sign of the number: A 1 bit indicates the number is negative; a 0 bit indicates the number is non-negative (i.e., zero or positive). Note that in the two's complement system, the bits to the right of the sign bit do *not* always represent the magnitude of the number. For example, 1111 in the two's complement system is −1. The three bits to the right of the sign bit, 111 (7 decimal), is *not* the magnitude of the number.

Signed and Unsigned Binary Numbers

If the number representation used for a number allows for positive and negative numbers, we say the number is a *signed number*. Otherwise it is an *unsigned number*. Because unsigned numbers have no sign, they represent only non-negative numbers. For example, the value of the unsigned number 1111 is 15 in decimal, but as a two's complement signed number, its value is −1. Note that the number 1111 can be either an unsigned number or a signed number.

What makes a binary number signed or unsigned is how it is treated. For example, suppose you compare 1111 and 0010 and conclude that 1111 is bigger (because 1111 represents 15 and 0010 represents 2). Then the numbers are unsigned because you are treating them that way. But if you conclude 0010 is bigger (because 0010 represents 2 and 1111 represents −1), then the numbers are signed.

From this point on, when we use the term "signed number," we mean a number in the two's complement system.

Range of Signed and Unsigned Binary Numbers

There are two patterns that can be represented by a single bit: either 0 or 1. With two bits, either bit can be 0 or 1. Thus, there are $2 \times 2 = 2^2 = 4$ patterns: 00, 01, 10, 11. With three bits, there are $2 \times 2 \times 2 = 2^3 = 8$ patterns: 000, 001, 010, 011, 100, 101, 110, 111. Generalizing, with n bits we get 2^n patterns.

If we represent unsigned numbers with four bits, we can have $2^4 = 16$ patterns. If we use these 2^4 patterns to represent the sequence of non-negative numbers starting with 0, we can represent the numbers 0 to $2^4 - 1$ (we go up to $2^4 - 1 = 15$, not 2^4, because we are starting from 0). Generalizing, with n bits we can represent unsigned numbers from 0 to $2^n - 1$. For example, with eight bits, we can represent unsigned numbers from 0 to $2^8 - 1 = 255$. The following table shows the values of all the four-bit signed and unsigned numbers:

Unsigned	Value	Signed	Value
0000	0	1000	-8
0001	1	1001	-7
0010	2	1010	-6
0011	3	1011	-5
0100	4	1100	-4
0101	5	1101	-3
0110	6	1110	-2
0111	7	1111	-1
1000	8	0000	0
1001	9	0001	1
1010	10	0010	2
1011	11	0011	3
1100	12	0100	4
1101	13	0101	5
1110	14	0110	6
1111	15	0111	7

With two's complement signed numbers, the left bit indicates the sign (0 for non-negative numbers or 1 or negative numbers). Suppose we represent numbers with four bits. For the negative numbers, the sign bit is 1, leaving only three bits to specify the negative number. With three bits, we can specify $2^3 = 8$ numbers. Thus, starting from -1, we can represent the numbers -1 down to -8. For the non-negative numbers, the sign bit is 0, leaving only three bits to specify the number. Thus, as with the negative numbers, we can represent $2^3 = 8$ non-negative numbers. But we start from 0, not 1. Thus, we can represent the numbers 0 to 7 (not 1 to 8). The table above shows the four-bit unsigned and signed numbers in ascending order along with their values in decimal. Note for the signed numbers, the negative numbers go down to -8, but the non-negative number go up to only $+7$. The numbers go one further in the negative direction than in the positive direction because the negative numbers start from -1, but the non-negative numbers start from 0.

The following table shows the ranges of unsigned and signed numbers with n bits for several values of n.

n	Unsigned	Signed
1	0 to 1	-1 to 0
2	0 to 3	-2 to 1
3	0 to 7	-4 to 3
4	0 to 15	-8 to 7
5	0 to 31	-16 to 15
6	0 to 63	-32 to 31
7	0 to 127	-64 to 63
8	0 to 255	-128 to 127
9	0 to 511	-256 to 255
10	0 to 1023	-512 to 511
12	0 to 4095	-2048 to 2047
16	0 to 65535	-32768 to 32767
k	0 to 2^k-1	-2^{k-1} to $2^{k-1}-1$

Do not attempt to memorize this table. Instead, learn the value of 2^n for n from 1 to 16. Once you know these powers of 2, it is easy to figure out the ranges of unsigned and signed numbers with n bits for the values of n in the table. For example, 8 bits has 256 patterns (because $2^8 = 256$). Thus, 8-bit unsigned numbers range from 0 to $2^8 - 1 = 255$. For signed numbers, half of the 2^8 patterns are for negative numbers, and half are for non-negative numbers. Half of 2^8 is $2^7 = 128$. Thus, 8-bit signed numbers range from -128 to 127. Here are the powers of 2 you should know:

n	2^n
1	2
2	4
3	8
4	16
5	32
6	64
7	128
8	256
9	512
10	1,024 (aka 1K)
11	2,048 (aka 2K)
12	4,096 (aka 4K)
15	32,768 (aka 32K)
16	65,536 (aka 64K)
20	1,048,576 (aka 1M)
30	1,073,741,824 (aka 1G)

Converting Between Binary and Hex

It is trivial to convert between binary and hex once you know the binary numbers from 0000 to 1111 and their hex equivalents. To convert a binary number to hex, break up the binary number into groups of four bits, starting from its right end. Then substitute the hex equivalent for each four-bit group. For example, to convert 11010111000001100, we first break it up into four-bit groups:

```
1   1010   1110   0000   1100
```

We then substitute the hex equivalent for each four-bit group:

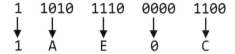

Thus, 11010111000001100 binary is equal to 1AE0C hex. To convert hex to binary, we simply substitute the four-bit binary equivalent for each hex digit. For example, to convert A5 to binary, substitute 1010 for A and 0101 for 5 to get 10100101.

Converting Decimal to Binary

If we repeatedly divide a number by 10 until we get a 0 quotient, the remainders will be the digits that represent that number in decimal. For example, let's divide 123 by 10 repeatedly:

```
                    remainders
                        ↓
            0   1
    10)     1   2
    10)    12   3
    10)   123        Start here and work up
```

As you can see, the remainders are the digits that make up the decimal number. If, instead, we repeatedly divide by 2, then the remainders will be the bits that make up the binary number equal to 123 decimal:

```
            0   1
    2)      1   1
    2)      3   1
    2)      7   1
    2)     15   0
    2)     30   1
    2)     61   1
    2)    123        Start here and work up
```

Reading the remainders from the top down, we get the bits that make up the binary number equal to 123 decimal. Thus, 123 decimal = 1111011 binary. Let's check our answer by converting it to hex and then to decimal. 1111011 = 111 1011 = 7B hex = 7×16 + 11 = 123 decimal. You can similarly convert numbers to hex by dividing repeatedly by 16.

Zero and Sign Extension

Suppose we have a one-byte binary number that we want to extend to two bytes (recall that a byte is eight bits). We can do this in two ways. We can add eight zeros on the left, or add eight copies of the sign bit on the left. For example, to extend 11111111, we can add eight zeros to get

    0000000011111111

or we can replicate the sign bit (i.e., its leftmost bit) of 11111111 to get

    1111111111111111

The former approach is called *zero extension*; the latter approach, *sign extension*.

If a negative signed number is zero-extended, it changes its value. 11111111 (which is equal to −1) zero-extended to 16 bits is 0000000011111111 (which is equal to +255). If, however, it is sign-extended, its value remains −1.

Rule: Always sign-extend signed numbers.

If an unsigned number with 1 in its leftmost position is sign-extended, its value changes. For example, if the unsigned number 11111111 (255) is sign-extended to 16 bits, we get 1111111111111111 (65535). However, if we zero-extend an unsigned number, its value remains the same.

Rule: Always zero-extend unsigned numbers.

Problems

1) Convert the following binary numbers to decimal:

    010111110110111, 011111111, 01000000000

2) Convert the binary numbers in the preceding problem to hex.

3) Add 8000 hex (−32768 decimal) and ffff hex (−1 decimal). Represent the computed result using 16 bits. What is the sign of the computed result? What is the sign of the true result? Why is there a discrepancy between the computed result and the true result?

4) What is the range of 12-bit unsigned numbers and 12-bit two's complement signed numbers?

5) What is the range of 5-bit two's complement numbers? 9-bit? 11-bit?

6) Convert the following decimal numbers to binary and hexadecimal:

    1023, 1024, 1025, 255, 16

7) Convert the following hexadecimal numbers to binary:

   5567 ABABAB, F03, 3579BDF, 2468ACE, FCC

8) Convert the following hexadecimal numbers to decimal:

   A0, B0, C0, D0, E0, F0, 400, 10000

9) Add the following pairs of binary numbers: Give your answers in both binary and hex.

```
0111111111111111       0111000111000111       0011111111111111
0000101010101011       0010101010101010       0000000000000001
```

10) Subtract the numbers in the preceding question.

11) Add the following pairs of hexadecimal numbers:

```
0FFFFFFF          996
000000001         959
```

12) Subtract the numbers in problem 11. Give your answers in both hex and decimal.

13) Write −75 decimal as a 16-bit two's complement binary number.

14) What is the next (and final number) in this sequence: 1000, 22, 20, 13, 12, 11, 10?

15) Convert 0.111 binary to decimal.

16) Convert 0.5 decimal to binary.

17) Convert 0.75 decimal to binary.

18) Convert 0.1 decimal to binary. *Hint*: Multiply repeatedly by 2, removing the whole part after each multiplication. The whole parts make up the binary number.

19) Convert the following octal (base 8) numbers to decimal: 123, 777, 100.

20) Convert the following base 9 numbers to octal (base 8): 123, 777, 100.

2 Machine Language

Introduction

Machine language is the only language the computer hardware can "understand." Thus, if you write a program in any language other than machine language, it first has to be translated to machine language before it can be executed by the computer. A machine language instruction is a binary number. A machine language program consists of a sequence of binary numbers.

Each type of computer has its own machine language. IBM mainframe computers have one type of machine language. PCs that run Windows have another type of machine language. In this book, we will study a RISC-V computer. RISC-V is an instruction set architecture—that is, it is essentially a description of a particular machine language. A RISC-V computer is any computer that conforms to this instruction set architecture.

RISC-V architecture specifies a base 32-bit integer architecture (called RV32I), a base 64-bit integer architecture (called RV64I), a base 128-bit integer architecture (called RV128I), and several extensions. In this book, we cover (and the software package supports) the RV32I base instruction set and the RV32M extension (multiplication and division instructions).

All the data, instructions, and addresses inside a computer are in binary. It is hard to read binary (for us—not for the computer), and binary numbers require a lot of space on the printed page. For this reason, after we complete our study of machine language in this chapter, we will generally use hexadecimal to represent the binary numbers within the RISC-V computer.

Structure of the RISC-V

The two principal units of the RISC-V are the *central processing unit* (CPU) and *main memory* (see the figure that follows). Within the CPU are the *arithmetic/logic unit* (ALU) and the *control unit*. The ALU is the unit that performs high-speed computations. The control unit is the control center for all the other components of the computer. Also, within the CPU are 32 storage areas, called *registers*, named x0, x1, ..., x31. Each of these registers can hold one 32-bit number. An additional register, the pc (program counter) register, "points to" the machine instruction in memory to be executed next.

Main memory of our computer (i.e., the computer that is simulated by the rv program in the software package for this book) has only $2^{16} = 65536$ cells, which is more than enough for our purposes. Each memory cell is one byte. That is, it can hold one 8-bit number. The memory cells are numbered starting with 0. The number of a cell (i.e., the number that identifies a particular cell) is called the *address* of that cell. The number *inside* a memory cell is the *contents* of that cell.

The *word size* of our RISC-V computer is 32 bits. That is, the computational circuits in the CPU operate on units of data that are 32 bits wide. For example, the adder circuit in the CPU can add two 32-bit numbers.

Each byte of memory has its own address. That is, successive addresses correspond to successive bytes. For this reason, we say its memory is *byte addressable*.

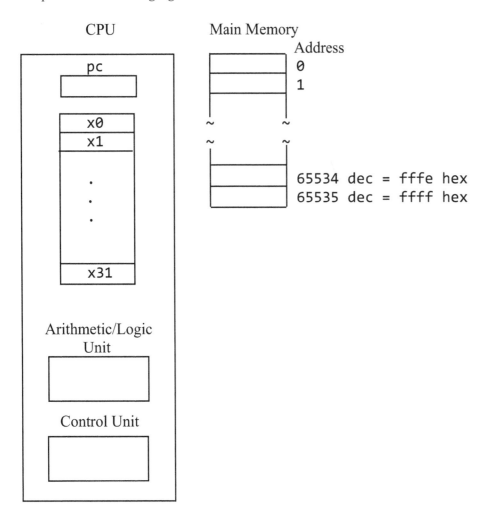

Each of the 32 registers x0 to x31 has an alias (an alternate name we can use). For example, x5 has the alias t0. The following table shows the alias of each of the 32 registers x0 to x31.

Register	Alias	Description
x0	zero	Read-only register containing 0
x1	ra	Return address
x2	sp	Stack pointer
x3	gp	Global pointer
x4	tp	Thread pointer
x5-x7	t0-t2	Temporary registers
x8-x9	s0-s1	Saved registers
x10-x11	a0-a1	Function arguments and returned values
x12-x17	a2-a7	Function arguments
x18-x27	s2-s11	Saved registers
x28-x31	t3-t6	Temporary registers

The *number of each register* is the number in its "x" name—not the number in its alias. For example, the number of x5 (which is also t0) is 5.

To execute a machine language program, the computer user enters a command to the operating system

(OS) specifying the name of the file that holds the machine language program. The OS responds by loading the program into memory starting at some address, referred to as the *load point*. To keep our discussion as simple as possible in this introduction, let's assume the load point is 0, and execution of the program starts at that address.

After the OS loads the program into main memory, it loads the pc register with the load point (we are assuming it is the address 0). The CPU then executes a loop which in its simplest form consists of four steps (a *loop* is a sequence of operations that are repeatedly executed):

1. *Fetch* the instruction the pc register "points to." That is, the CPU fetches the instruction in main memory whose address is in the pc register. The CPU does not remove the instruction from main memory. Instead, it makes a copy of it. Thus, the contents of the location in main memory that the pc register points to are unaffected.

2. Add 4 to the pc register.

3. *Decode* instruction.

4. *Execute* the instruction fetched in step 1.

The first time the steps in the loop are executed, the pc register contains 0. Thus, in step 1, the CPU fetches the instruction from main memory that is at the address 0. In step 2, it increments the pc register to 4. Each instruction in four bytes long. Thus, step 2 modifies the pc so it points to the next instruction in main memory. In step 3, it *decodes* the instruction (i.e., determines its opcode and accesses its operands). In step 4, it executes the instruction it fetched in step 1. On the next iteration of the loop, the CPU fetches the instruction at the address 4—not 0—because the pc register now contains 4 (because of step 2 in the preceding iteration). Each time the CPU performs step 1, it gets the next instruction from main memory because step 2 in the preceding iteration adds 4 to the pc register. Thus, the CPU executes instructions one after another in order of memory address. This process continues until a halt, branch, or jump machine instruction is executed. A halt machine instruction halts the execution of the program and causes a return to the OS. A branch or jump machine instruction does not halt execution. Instead, it causes the CPU to go to a new location and start executing instructions from there. For example, a branch instruction at address 12 can cause the CPU to go back to address 0 and execute instructions in memory order starting again from there. *Note*: We will generally refer to main memory simply as "memory."

Simple Machine Language Program

Let's introduce some terminology. Consider the following arithmetic expression:

$2 + 3$

The *operation* is addition. The symbol "+" is the *operator*. The numbers 2 and 3 are the *operands* used in the operation. An *opcode* in a machine instruction is a code that specifies the operation that the CPU is to perform. A *destination register* is a register that is to receive the result of an operation. A *source register* is a register that provides the CPU with an operand or addressing information on an operand. An *immediate value* is a value within a machine instruction. When the CPU fetches an instruction that contains an immediate value, the CPU has immediate access to that value (because the CPU already has the instruction that contains the immediate value)—hence, the name "immediate value."

Let's now examine a simple machine language program. It consists of six instructions, each occupying one word (i.e., four bytes) in memory, and two data words. Let's assume this program is loaded into memory starting at the address 0. Here is a description and the address of each word in the program:

Address (hex)	Description of Instruction
0:	Load the constant 2 from memory location 14 hex into the t0 (x5) register.
4:	Load the constant 3 from memory location 18 hex into the t1 (x6) register.
8:	Add the contents of t0 and t1 and load t0 with the sum, overlaying the constant 2.
c:	Display in decimal the sum in t0 on the display monitor.
10:	Halt.
14:	Constant 2.
18:	Constant 3.

The instruction at address 0 is a lw (load word) instruction. Here is a diagram that shows its format:

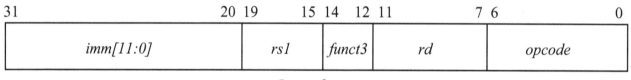

I-type format

The *funct3* field together with the *opcode* field specify the operation the CPU is to perform. For a lw instruction, the *funct3* field is 101 and the opcode field is 0000011. The *rd field* specifies the number of the destination register. In the lw instruction, the destination register is the register that receives the word loaded from memory. We want a lw instruction that loads t0. t0 is the alias for x5. Thus, the number of the t0 register in binary is 00101 (5 decimal), and therefore the *rd* field in our lw instruction should be 00101 (5 decimal). The *rs1 field* specifies a source register. In the lw instruction, the *rs1* field together with the immediate value in the *imm[11:0]* field provides the address of the word that is to be loaded from memory. The bracketed expression, *[11:0]*, indicates that the field contains 12 bits numbered 11 to 0, left to right. The *effective address* (i.e., the 32-bit memory address that the computer uses to access memory) is given by

(the contents of the register specified by the *rs1* field) + (the value in the *imm[11:0]* field).

Here in binary is the lw instruction we need at the start of our program:

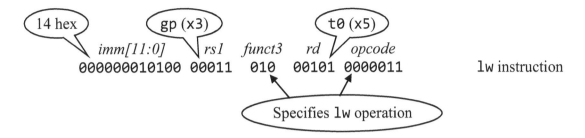

lw instruction

The value in the *rd* field, 00101 (5 decimal), is the number of the t0 register. Thus, this instruction loads the t0 register. The value in the *rs1* field, 00011 (3 decimal), is the number of the x3 register whose alias is gp (global pointer). When we run this program, the gp register will contain zero. Thus, the effective address is given by just the value in the *imm[11:0]* field, which is equal to 14 hex. At location 14 hex in our program is the constant 2. Thus, this lw instruction loads 2 into t0.

The next instruction in our program is another lw instruction:

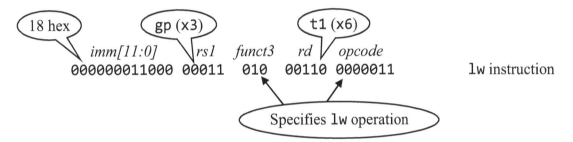

lw instruction

It is identical to the first lw instruction except that its *imm[11:0]* fields contains 18 hex and its *rd* field contains the number of the t1 register. At location 18 hex in our program is the constant 3. Thus, this instruction loads 3 into t1.

The next instruction is an add instruction. It has a format that is different than the format of the lw instruction. The format of the lw instruction is the *I-type format* ("I" for "immediate). The format for an add instruction is the *R-type format* ("R" for "register"). It specifies a second source register with its *rs2* field. Its operation is specified by three fields: the seven-bit *funct7* field, the three-bit *funct3* field, and the seven-bit *opcode* field. Here is the R-type format:

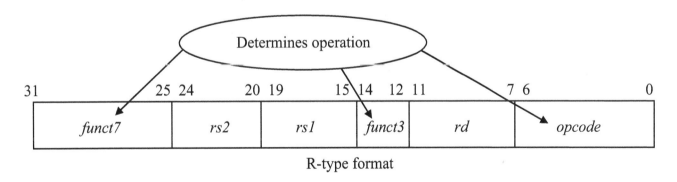

R-type format

For our program, we want an add instruction that adds the contents of t0 and t1, and loads the sum into t0. Here is the add instruction we need:

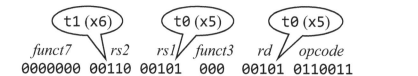

funct7 \ *rs2*   *rs1*/ *funct3*   *rd* / *opcode*
0000000 00110 00101   000   00101 0110011   add instruction

The add instruction has three register fields: *rs1*, *rs2*, and *rd*. When executed, it adds the contents of the registers specified by the *rs1* and *rs2* fields, and loads the sum into the register specified by the *rd* field. The *rs1* field in this instruction is 00101 (5 decimal). It specifies x5 (which is also t0). The *rs2* field is 00110 (6 decimal). It specifies x6 (which is also t1). The *rd* field is 00101 (5 decimal). It specifies x5 (which is also t0). Thus, when executed, this instruction adds the contents of t0 and t1, and loads the sum into t0, overlaying the constant 2 loaded there by our first lw instruction. The operation for this instruction is specified by the *funct7*, *funct3*, and the *opcode* fields.

The next instruction is the dout (decimal out) instruction. The dout instruction uses the R-type format, but it does not use its *rs2* or *rd* fields:

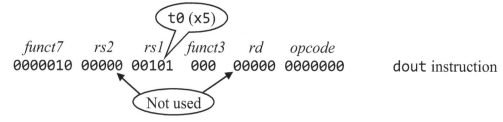

funct7   *rs2*   *rs1*/ *funct3*   *rd*   *opcode*
0000010 00000 00101   000   00000 0000000   dout instruction

It converts a copy of the binary value in the register specified by the *rs1* field to decimal and displays it on the display monitor. The *rs1* field in the instruction above is 00101 (5 decimal). Thus, it specifies x5 (which is also t0). When executed, it displays in decimal the contents of t0.

The final instruction in a program is the halt instruction, which terminates execution of the program. It contains all zeros:

funct7   *rs2*   *rs1*   *funct3*   *rd*   *opcode*
0000000 00000 00000   000   00000 0000000   halt instruction

Note: How to halt a program or perform an I/O operation on a computer is generally highly dependent on the operating system. Moreover, performing even simple I/O operations can require a complex sequence of instructions. Assembly language programmers often avoid the difficulty of using I/O instructions by calling pre-written I/O subroutines (such as the printf and scanf functions in the C standard library). In this book, we have an even easier approach. To halt a program or do I/O, we use a set of simple, system independent, and high-level instructions, all of which are supported by the rv program in the software package for this book (see the RISC-V summary in Appendix B). But be advised, these instructions (dout, the other I/O instructions, and halt) are not RISC-V instructions. They are supported only by the rv program. These "fake" instructions are easy to identify: They all have 0000000 in their *opcode* fields.

Following the halt instruction are our two data words:

00000000000000000000000000000010 (2 decimal)
00000000000000000000000000000011 (3 decimal)

The text file r0201.bin in the software package for this book contains our complete machine language program. Here are its contents:

```
                        r0201.bin
┌──────────────────────────────────────────────────────────┐
│ 000000010100 00011 010 00101 0000011    # lw              │
│ 000000011000 00011 010 00110 0000011    # lw              │
│ 0000000 00110 00101 000 00101 0110011   # add             │
│ 0000010 00000 00101 000 00000 0000000   # dout            │
│ 0000000 00000 00000 000 00000 0000000   # halt            │
│ 00000000000000000000000000000010        # data (2)        │
│ 00000000000000000000000000000011        # data (3)        │
└──────────────────────────────────────────────────────────┘
```

On the right of each line, we have added a comment that describes that line (comments start with the "#" character and extend to the end of the line). To run this program using the rv program in the software package for this book, first invoke the Command Prompt program (on Windows) or the Terminal program (on OS X, Linux, or Raspbian). Next, position the operating system on the directory that contains the software package for this book. Do this with the cd command. Then enter on the command line

        rv r0201.bin   (on Windows)
or
        ./rv r0201.bin   (on OS X, Linux, or Raspbian)

Note: On a Mac OS X, Linux, or Raspbian system, if the operating system responds with "command not found," enter on the command line

        chmod 755 *

and then re-enter the rv command. The chmod command allows programs in the software package to be executed.

The rv program inputs the r0201.bin file and outputs it, converted to executable form, to the file r0201.e, and then executes the program in r0201.e.

Note: The first time you run the rv program, it will prompt you for your name so it can include it in the list files it creates.

When you run r0201.bin with rv, you will see on your display the following:

```
┌──────────────────────────────────────────────────────────┐
│ rv Version 3.4 Copyright (c) 2019 by Anthony J. Dos Reis  │
│ 5                                                          │
└──────────────────────────────────────────────────────────┘
```

Following the copyright line is the output produced by our machine language program. Our program adds 2 and 3 and displays the sum. Thus, the output is 5, as expected. In addition to displaying the output produced by our program, rv creates three output files: r0201.e, r0201.lst, and r0201.bst. The file r0201.e holds the executable form of the program; r0201.lst is a time-stamped text file that shows the date and time of the run, your name, the header in r0201.e, each instruction of the program in hex form along with its location, the output, and some statistics on the program. The r0201.bst file is identical to the r0201.lst file except in the former the machine language program is displayed in binary. Here is r0201.lst file:

```
                                    r0201.lst
┌─────────────────────────────────────────────────────────────────────┐
│ rv Version 3.4                          Mon Jul  8 11:07:07 2019      │
│ Anthony J. Dos Reis                                                   │
│                                                                       │
│ Header                                                                │
│ R ◄─── file signature                                                 │
│ C ◄─── indicates the end of the header                                │
│                                                                       │
│ Loc    Code                                                           │
│ 0000   0141a283 ⎞                                                     │
│ 0004   0181a303 ⎟                                                     │
│ 0008   006282b3 ⎬    Instructions in hex                             │
│ 000c   04028000 ⎟                                                     │
│ 0010   00000000 ⎠                                                     │
│ 0014   00000002 ⎫   Data in hex                                      │
│ 0018   00000003 ⎭                                                     │
│ ================================================== Output            │
│ 5                                                                     │
│ =============================================== Program statistics   │
│ Input file name      = r0201.bin                                     │
│ Instructions executed = 5 (decimal)                                  │
│ Program size         = 1c (hex) 28 (decimal)                         │
│ Load point           = 0 (hex) 0 (decimal)                           │
│ Programmer           = Anthony J. Dos Reis                           │
└─────────────────────────────────────────────────────────────────────┘
```

An executable file consists of two parts: a *header* and a code part (the code part is sometimes referred to as the *text*). The header in the executable file r0201.e contains the letter R followed by the letter C (see the listing above). The letter R indicates that the file is a machine code file created by the rv program. We call the letter R the *signature* of rv files. The letter C marks the end of the header.

Alternatively, we can run our program with the trace feature of the rv program active. To do this, enter on the command line

>   rv r0201.bin -t   (on Windows)

or

>   ./rv r0201.bin -t   (on OS X, Linux, or Raspbian)

The rv program will then display the following:

```
rv Version 3.4 Copyright (c) 2019 by Anthony J. Dos Reis
================================================================
   0: 0141a283      # lw
     <t0 = 0/2>
   4: 0181a303      # lw
     <t1 = 0/3>
   8: 006282b3      # add
     <t0 = 2/5>
   c: 04028000      # dout

5
  10: 00000000      # halt
```

Each instruction is displayed in hex form as it is executed along with its location in memory and effect. For example,

```
   0: 0141a283      # lw
     <t0 = 0/2>
```

indicates that the `lw` instruction, 0141a283, at location 0 changed the contents of `t0` from 0 to 2 (the slash separates the "before" value from the "after" value).

A third alternative is to run the `rv` program with the debugger active. To do this, enter

```
     rv r0201.bin -d
```
(on Windows)

or

```
     ./rv r0201.bin -d
```
(on OS X, Linux, or Raspbian)

The `rv` program will then execute and trace one instruction each time you hit the Enter key. You can change the number of instructions executed each time you hit the Enter key. For example, to change to two instructions per Enter key, enter 2 at the prompt. Then thereafter, two instructions are executed each time you hit the enter key. In the following example, we hit Enter twice, each time resulting in the execution of one instruction. We then enter 2, resulting the execution of two instructions each time we hit the Enter key:

```
lw>>>  ─────────────⟨  Hit Enter key here  ⟩
    0: 0141a283        ; lw
       <t0 = 0/2>  ─⟨  Hit Enter key here  ⟩
lw>>>
    4: 0181a303        ; lw
       <t1 = 0/3>  ─⟨  Change to 2 instructions per Enter  ⟩
add>>> 2 ─┘
    8: 006282b3        ; add ⎫
       <t0 = 2/5>            ⎬  Now two instructions executed per Enter
    c: 04028000        ; dout⎭

5
        ─⟨  Hit Enter key here  ⟩
halt>>>
   10: 00000000        ; halt
```

Creating files like `r0201.bin` that contain the binary form of a machine language program can be tedious because 32 keystrokes are required for each instruction. Alternatively, we can represent a machine language program in hex. For example, the file `r0201.hex` contains the program in `r0201.bin` but in hex form:

```
            r0201.hex
┌──────────────────────────┐
│ 0141a283    # lw         │
│ 0181a303    # lw         │
│ 006282b3    # add        │
│ 04028000    # dout       │
│ 00000000    # halt       │
│ 00000002    # data (2)   │
│ 00000003    # data (3)   │
└──────────────────────────┘
```

We can run this file on `rv` the same way we run the `r0201.bin` file. For example, to run the program in `r0201.hex`, enter

        rv r0201.hex   (on Windows)
or
        ./rv r0201.hex   (on OS X, Linux, Raspbian)

Rule: File names of the text files that contain the binary form of machine language instructions must end with the extension ".bin". Names of the text files with the hex form must end with the extension ".hex".

Rule: In ".bin" files, spaces embedded in the machine language instructions are allowed, but not in the ".hex" files.

To create your own ".bin" and ".hex" files you must use a text editor—not a word processor. A simple text editor available on Windows is `notepad`. For example, to create a file named `sample.bin` on a Windows system, first activate the `Command Prompt` program, and position the OS on the directory that has the software package for this book. Then enter on the command line

```
notepad sample.bin
```

On an OS X, Linux, or Raspbian system, first activate the `Terminal` program, and position the OS on the directory that has the software package for this book. Then enter on the command line

```
nano sample.bin
```

Non-Zero Load Point

Before a machine language program can be executed, the operating system must load it into main memory from some I/O device such as a hard disk drive. The starting memory address at which a program is loaded is called its *load point*:

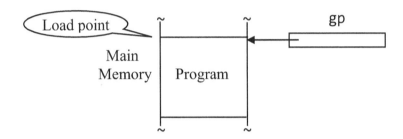

When the `rv` program (which acts like the operating system) loads a program into memory, it initializes the `gp` register with the load point (we indicate this in the diagram above by showing an arrow emanating from the `gp` register pointing to the load point). Thus, if the load point is 0, the `gp` register is initialized with 0. If, however, the load point is 300 hex, then the `gp` register is initialized with 300 hex. Recall that the constant 2 in the program in `r0201.bin` is at the address 14 hex *relative to the beginning of the program*. Thus, if the program is loaded starting at location 0, the constant 2 is at the memory address 14 hex. But if the program is loaded starting at location 300 hex, then the constant 2 is at the address 314 hex. But in both cases, the `lw` instructions in `r0201.bin` will *correctly* access the constants 2 and 3. Recall that the effective address that an `lw` instruction uses when it fetches a constant from memory is given by the contents of the `gp` register plus the immediate value in the instruction. Thus, if the load point is 0, the effective address used by the first `lw` instruction is

(contents of **gp**) + (immediate value in `lw` instruction) = 0 + 14 hex = 14 hex

which is the address of the constant 2 in memory. But if the load point is 300 hex, then the effective address is

(contents of **gp**) + (immediate value in `lw` instruction) = 300 hex + 14 hex = 314 hex

which is the address of the constant 2 in memory when the load point is 300 hex. Regardless of the load point, the first `lw` instruction always loads the constant 2. Similarly, the second `lw` instruction always loads 3 regardless of the load point.

Important point: The immediate value in a `lw` instruction is the address of the operand to be loaded relative to the beginning of the program. The `gp` register provides the address of the beginning of the program. Thus, the `gp` register contents together with the immediate value provide the address of the operand in memory regardless of the load point. Because the immediate value is a *relative* address, it does not have to be adjusted depending on the load point.

By default, the `rv` program loads programs into memory starting at the address 0. However, we can specify any load point we want when we invoke `rv` using the `-L` command line argument (in either upper of lower case). For example, to run `r0201.bin` with a load point of 300 hex, enter

```
         rv r0201.bin -L 300          (on Windows)
or
         ./rv r0201.bin -L 300        (on OS X, Linux, or Raspbian)
```

Add Immediate Instruction

The program we discussed in the preceding section uses a three-instruction sequence (`lw, lw, add`) to add 2 and 3. However, we can get the same result with a more efficient two-instruction sequence: an `addi` (add immediate) instruction that loads `t0` with 2, and a second `addi` instruction that adds 3 to `t0`. Neither instruction accesses any constants in memory. The `addi` instruction uses the I-type format, just like the `lw` instruction. Here is the first `addi` instruction:

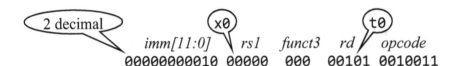

```
   2 decimal          x0                    t0
              imm[11:0]  \ rs1    funct3    rd /  opcode
              00000000010 00000    000     00101 0010011
```

When executed, it adds the contents of the *rs1* register and the *imm[11:0]* value, and loads the sum into the register specified by the *rd* field. In the instruction above, the *rs1* field specifies the `x0` register—a register that *permanently contains 0*. Thus, for the instruction above, the computed sum is 0 plus the *imm[11:0]* value, which of course is equal to just the *imm[11:0]* value. Thus, the instruction simply loads the *imm[11:0]* value (equal to 2 decimal in this instruction), after sign-extending it to 32 bits, into the register specified by the *rd* field (the `t0` register in this instruction). Note that the value loaded into `t0` comes from the instruction itself (from the *imm[11:0]* field). Thus, as soon as the CPU fetches the instruction, the value to be loaded into `t0` is immediately available to the CPU. Unlike the `lw` instruction, the execution of the `addi` instruction does not need to fetch from memory the value to be loaded. Instructions like the `addi` instruction are called *immediate instructions* because the operand needed for the computation *is in the instruction itself*, and therefore is immediately available to the CPU—hence, the name "immediate instruction."

The second `addi` instruction in our program is like the first except that the *rs1* field specifies `t0` (`x5`), and the immediate value is 3:

```
                  t0                    t0
        imm[11:0]  \ rs1    funct3    rd /  opcode
        00000000011 00101    000     00101 0010011
```

Thus, it adds the contents of `t0` (which is 2) with the immediate value (3) and loads the sum into the *rd* register (which is also `t0`).

To complete the program, we need a `dout` instruction and a `halt`. Here is the complete program:

```
                         r0202.bin
000000000010 00000 000 00101 0010011    # addi, loads t0 with 2
000000000011 00101 000 00101 0010011    # addi, adds 3 to t0
0000010 00000 00101 000 00000 0000000   # dout, displays t0
0000000 00000 00000 000 00000 0000000   # halt, terminates execution
```

Our `r0202.bin` program is better than our `r0201.bin` program in two respects: It takes less space (four words versus seven) and executes more quickly. Instructions like `lw` that access memory typically take longer to execute than instructions that do not access memory. Thus, if `r0202.bin` requires four units of time to execute (one unit for each instruction), `r0201.bin` would probably require more than 5 units of time although it has only one more instruction than `r0202.bin`.

The `addi` instruction is a versatile instruction. We can use it to add a number to a register. For example, if its *rs1* and *rd* fields both specify `t0`, and its immediate field holds 5, it adds 5 to `t0`. We can also use an `addi` instruction to initialize a register to a number. For example, if its *rs1* specifies `x0`, its *rd* field specifies `t0`, and its immediate field holds 5, it initializes `t0` with 5. A third use of the `addi` instruction is to move (i.e., copy) the contents of one register to another register. For example, if its *rs1* field specifies `t0`, its *rd* field specifies `t1`, and its immediate field contains 0, it copies the contents of `t0` into `t1`, after which `t0` and `t1` will have identical contents.

Store Word Instruction

The `sw` (store word) instructions does the reverse of the `lw` instruction. A `lw` instruction loads a register with a word from memory; a `sw` instruction stores a word from a register into a memory location. Because the `sw` instruction does not load a register, it does not have a *rd* field (recall that the *rd* field specifies the destination register—the register that receives the result of an operation). But the `sw` instruction has a *rs2* field that specifies the register whose contents the `sw` instruction stores in memory. The register specified by the *rs1* field along with the immediate value provides the effective address—the address of the memory location that receives the value stored—given by:

$$\text{effective address} = (\text{contents of the } rs1 \text{ register}) + \text{immediate value}$$

The `sw` instruction uses the S-type format:

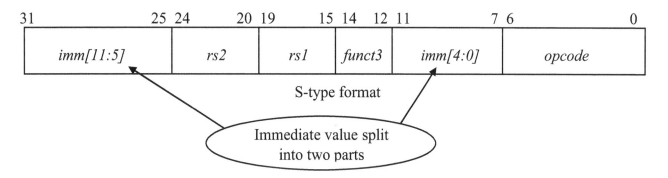

S-type format

Immediate value split into two parts

For engineering reasons (specifically, so that register access can start before instruction decoding), the placement of the register fields within an instruction should be the same across the entire instruction set. For example, the *rs2* field in the add instruction is in bit positions 24 to 20. Thus, it should be in those positions in all the instructions in which it is present. Because of this constraint, the immediate value in a sw instruction has to be split into two parts because of the presence of the *rs2* field. One part is in bit positions 31 to 25 of the instruction (which is normally the *funct7* field). The other part is in bits positions 11 to 7 of the instruction (which is normally the *rd* field).

Let's write a three-word program that stores the contents of the sp register into memory. The first word is a sw instruction, the second is a halt instruction, and the third is the location that receives the value stored:

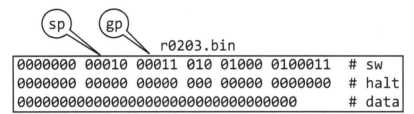

```
            r0203.bin
0000000 00010 00011 010 01000 0100011    # sw
0000000 00000 00000 000 00000 0000000    # halt
00000000000000000000000000000000         # data
```

The *rs2* field in the sw instruction contains 00010, the number of the sp register. Thus, the sw instruction stores the contents of the sp register. The immediate value consists of the seven bits in the *funct7* field position (0000000) concatenated to the five bits in the *rd* field position (01000). Thus, the immediate value is 000000001000 (8 decimal). The *rs1* field contains 00011, the number of the gp register. Thus, the effective address—the address of the location that receives the value stored—is given by the contents of the gp register (which will contain the load point when the program is executed) plus the immediate value 8. Thus, the location that receives the value stored is 8 bytes above the load point. The sw instruction is at the load point. Thus, the location that receives the value stored is 8 bytes after the sw instruction, which corresponds to the third word of the program.

Let's run the program in r0203.bin to see if it stores the contents of the sp register into its third word. Enter

       rv r0203.bin -m -x   (on Windows)

or

       ./rv r0203.bin -m -x   (on OS X, Linux, or Raspbian)

The -m and -x command line arguments cause the rv program to display the contents of memory and the contents of the registers, respectively, when the halt instruction is executed. Here is what you will see on the screen:

```
rv Version 3.4 Copyright (c) 2019 by Anthony J. Dos Reis

------------------------------------------------- Memory display
0000: 0021a423
0004: 00000000
0008: 00010000
--------------------------------------------- End of memory display


-------------------------------------------------- Register display
pc  = 00000008
x0  = 00000000    ra  = 00000000    sp  = 00010000    gp  = 00000000
tp  = 00000000    t0  = 00000000    t1  = 00000000    t2  = 00000000
s0  = 00000000    s1  = 00000000    a0  = 00000000    a1  = 00000000
a2  = 00000000    a3  = 00000000    a4  = 00000000    a5  = 00000000
a6  = 00000000    a7  = 00000000    s2  = 00000000    s3  = 00000000
s4  = 00000000    s5  = 00000000    s6  = 00000000    s7  = 00000000
s8  = 00000000    s9  = 00000000    s10 = 00000000    s11 = 00000000
t3  = 00000000    t4  = 00000000    t5  = 00000000    t6  = 00000000
------------------------------------------- End of register display
```

(annotations: "halt instruction" points to `0004: 00000000`; an arrow connects `0008: 00010000` and `sp = 00010000`)

From the register display, we can see that the contents of the sp register is 00010000. From the memory display, we can confirm that the sw stored the contents of the sp register was indeed stored into the location in memory right after the halt instruction.

We can also determine what happens when we run r0203.bin using the debugger in the rv program. To run rv and activate the debugger, enter

```
        rv  r0203.bin -d
```
or
```
        ./rv r0203.bin -d
```

Then hit the Enter key to execute the sw instruction. You will see on the screen,

```
rv Version 3.4 Copyright (c) 2019 by Anthony J. Dos Reis
================================================================
sw>>>    0: 0021a423       ; sw
        mem[8] = 0/10000
```

We can see that the effect of the sw instruction is to change memory location 8 from 0 to 10000. To confirm this, enter m8 to display memory location 8:

```
halt>>> m8
0008: 00010000
```

The prompt, `halt>>>`, indicates that the next instruction to be executed is a `halt` instruction. The `m` debugger command does not execute the current expression—it simply displays the memory location specified. Thus, after displaying location 0008, the debugger repeats the `halt>>` prompt. To confirm that 00010000 is in the `sp` register, display the contents of the `sp` register by entering `xsp`:

```
halt>>> xsp
sp = 00010000
```

To execute the next (and last) instruction in this example, hit Enter.

When the debugger is active, to display a register enter `x` followed by the register name or number. To display all the registers, enter just `x`. To execute to the end of the program without pausing further for the debugger, enter `g` (for go to end).

Note: At this point, you may be suffering from information overload—from too much information on instruction formats. But actually, what you need to know is not much at all:

- The register specified by the *rd* field is always the register that receives the result of the operation.

- Instructions, like `lw`, `addi`, and `sw` that access or store an operand in memory, the effective address (i.e., the 32-bit address the computer uses to access the memory location) is given by the

  > address in the register specified by the *rs1* field
  > +
  > the immediate value in the instruction.

- In almost all the instructions that have a *rs2* field (i.e., all the R-type instructions), the *rs2* field specifies one of the registers that holds an operand. The *rs1* field specifies the register that holds the other operand. For example, the `add` instruction has a *rs1* field and a *rs2* field These fields specify the registers whose contents are to be added.

- In *one and only one* instruction—the `sw` instruction—the register specified by *rs2* field has a different function: It specifies the register whose contents are to be stored in memory. It is the "source" of the store operation. Thus, esthetically (and for engineering reasons), it makes sense to use the source register field *rs2* to specify the register whose contents are to be stored.

Not much at all! And furthermore, you have the RISC-V summary in Appendix B at your disposal to provide you with the specifics on any instruction.

Branch Instructions

Machine instructions are normally executed serially in order of increasing memory address. For example, after the machine instruction at address 0 is executed, the machine instruction at address 4 is executed, then the machine instruction at address 8, and so on. However, a branch instruction can change this execution pattern. It does this by loading a new value into the `pc` register. When it does this, we say that it is *transferring control* to a new location in memory. Recall that the CPU executes a loop that repeatedly

1. fetches the instruction that the `pc` register points to
2. increments the `pc` register (so it is pointing to the next instruction in memory)
3. decodes the instruction
4. executes the instruction it just fetched.

For example, suppose the `pc` register contains 10 hex, and at this address is a branch instruction. The CPU fetches the branch instruction at address 10, increments the `pc` to 14, decodes the instruction, and then executes the instruction. When the branch instruction is executed, it can change the address in the `pc` register. For example, it can change the address in the `pc` register to 0. Then when the CPU proceeds to fetch the next instruction, it fetches the instruction at the address 0—not at the address 14—because the `pc` register now contains 0.

All the instructions that the `rv` program supports are one-word (i.e., 32-bit) instructions. However, a RISC-V computer can also have half-word (i.e., 16-bit) instructions (the RV32C extension). A one-word instruction is required to start on a word boundary—that is, at an address that is a multiple of 4 (which means the address in binary ends with at least two 0's). A half-word instruction is required to start on a halfword boundary—that is, at an address that is a multiple of 2 (which means the address in binary ends with at least one zero). Thus, any time a branch occurs, the address of the branch instruction and the branch-to address both must have a zero in at least its rightmost bit. The *offset* (sometimes called the *displacement*) in a branch instruction is the difference between the branch-to address and the address of the branch instruction. For example, if a branch instruction at location 100 branches to location 108, then the offset is $108 - 100 = 8$. Offsets can also be negative. For example, if the branch instruction at location 104 branches to location 100, then the offset is $100 - 104 = -4$. Because both the branch-to address and the address of the branch instruction are divisible by 2, their difference—which is the offset—is also divisible by 2. Thus, *the rightmost bit of the offset has to be 0.*

The branch instructions use *pc-relative addresses*. That is, the branch-to address is given by the address in the `pc` when the branch instruction is fetched plus an offset which is provided by the immediate value in the branch instruction. For example, suppose a branch instruction is at the address 104 in memory, and the offset is -4. Then the branch-to address is

(address in the `pc` register when the branch instruction is fetched) + (-4)

The address in the `pc` register when the branch instruction is fetched is, of course, the address of the branch instruction. Thus, the branch-to address is

$$104 + (-4) = 100$$

The address 100 is the address of the instruction that immediately precedes the branch instruction. Thus, this branch, if it occurs, is to that instruction.

A branch instruction specifies two source registers (but no destination register) and an operation that requires the *funct3* field and the *opcode* field. Thus, the 7-bit *funct7* field and the 5-bit *rd* field—for a total of 12 bits—provide a 12-bit immediate field to hold the offset. As we already mentioned, for engineering reasons, the placement of the register fields within an instruction should be same across the instruction set. For example, the *rs2* field in the `add` instruction is in bit positions 24 to 20. Thus, in a branch instruction it *should also occupy the same positions*. Because of this constraint, the immediate field in a branch instruction has to be split into two parts: One part in bit positions 31 to 25 in the instruction (which is normally the *funct7* field), and one part in bit positions 11 to 7 (which is normally the *rd* field):

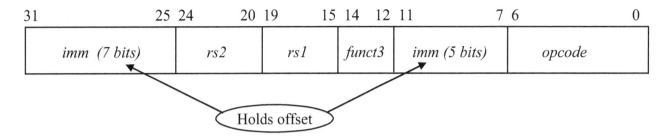

Because the rightmost bit of the offset is always 0, it does not have to be stored in the instruction. Thus, with the 12 bits available in the *funct7* and *rd* fields, we store bits 12 to 1 of the offset, but not bit 0 (i.e., the rightmost bit) of the offset. Accordingly, you would expect the *funct7* field to hold bits 12 to 6 of the offset, and the *rd* field to hold bits 5 to 1:

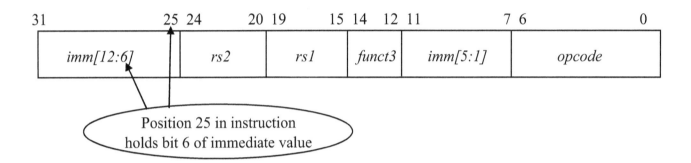

With this format, position 25 of the instruction holds bit 6 of the immediate value. But position 25 in all the non-branching instructions with a 12-bit immediate field (i.e., the I-type instructions) holds bit 5—not bit 6—of the immediate value. Thus, for consistency sake, position 25 in a branch instruction should also hold bit 5 of the offset, resulting in positions 26, 27, 28, 29, 30, and 31 in a branch instruction holding bits 6, 7, 8, 9, 10, and 11 of the offset. But where then do we put bit 12 of the offset? We could put bit 12 in the *rd* field along with bits 4 to 1. But for engineering reasons, it is important for the sign bit (i.e., leftmost bit) of an immediate value to be in the same position across the instruction set. In all the non-branch instructions, the sign bit of the immediate value is in position 31 in the instruction. Thus, in a branch instruction, it should also be in position 31. But bit 11 of the immediate value is there. Thus, we have to move bit 11 in the immediate value to the *rd* field to make room for bit 12. The result is the following format for the branch instruction:

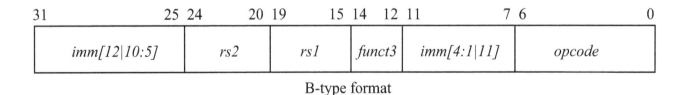

B-type format

In the diagram above, *imm[12|10:5]* in the *funct7* field position indicates that the field consists of bit 12 of the offset followed by bits 10 to 5. *imm[4:1|11]* in the *rd* field position indicates that the field consists of bits 4 to 1 of the offset followed by bit 11.

There are six branch instructions:

1. beq (branch if the contents of the *rs1* and *rs2* registers are equal)
2. bne (branch if the contents of the *rs1* and *rs2* registers are not equal)
3. blt (branch if the contents of the *rs1* register are less than the contents of the *rs2* register, signed number comparison)
4. bge (branch if the contents of the *rs1* register are greater than or equal to the contents of the *rs2* register, signed number comparison)
5. bltu (branch if the contents of the *rs1* register are less than the contents of the *rs2* register, unsigned number comparison)
6. bgeu (branch if the contents of the *rs1* register are greater than or equal to the contents of the *rs2* register, unsigned number comparison)

Each branch instruction compares the two registers specified by its *rs1* and *rs2* fields. If the condition tested holds, the branch occurs. For example, the beq instruction branches if the contents of the *rs1* and *rs2* registers are equal. If, however, the condition does not hold, then the instruction in memory that follows the branch instruction is executed next.

blt and bge treat the numbers in the *rs1* and *rs2* registers as signed numbers. bltu and bgeu perform the corresponding tests but treat the numbers as unsigned numbers. For example, suppose t1 contains -1 (ffffffff hex) and t2 contains 2. Then a blt instruction whose *rs1* and *rs2* registers are t1 and t2, respectively, would branch because -1 in t1 is less than 2 in t2. But a bltu instruction with the same registers would not branch because ffffffff hex in t1 is not less than 2 in t2 when the contents of the two registers are treated as unsigned numbers (ffffffff hex as an unsigned number is approximately four billion).

Now that we know the format of the branch instructions and how they work, let's write a machine language program that repeatedly displays in hex the value in the gp register. The program consists of two instructions:

1. hout instruction that displays the contents of the gp register in hex
2. beq (branch on equal) instruction that branches back to the hout instruction

The hout (hex out) instruction works like the dout instruction except that it displays in hex, not in decimal. Because the beq instruction branches back to the hout instruction, the hout and beq instruction are executed repeatedly. We call a sequence of instructions that is executed repeatedly a *loop*. The loop in our two-instruction program never stops executing. So we call it an *infinite loop*. However, it will not really execute forever. When the rv program detects that an excessive number of instructions have been executed, it pauses and allows the user to quit, use the debugger, or continue execution.

Here is the hout instruction we need:

```
 funct7     rs2     rs1   funct3    rd     opcode
0000100   00000   00011    000    00000   0000000
```

Its opcode is 0000000, which indicates it is an I/O instruction or the halt instruction. Its *funct7* field is 0000100, which identifies it as the hout instruction. Its *rs1* field is 00011 (3 decimal). Thus, it specifies register x3, whose alias is gp. This instruction displays the contents of the gp register in hex.

Here is the beq instruction we need:

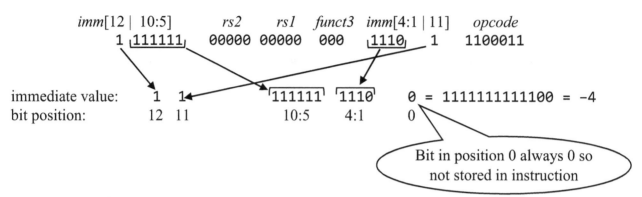

The beq instruction compares the contents of the *rs1* and *rs2* registers. Because the instruction above specifies the same register (x0) in the *rs1* and *rs2* fields, the test for equality performed by the beq instruction necessarily produces a true result. Thus, the instruction always branches. The immediate value is equal to −4. The beq instruction branches to the address given by its address plus the immediate value (because it uses pc-relative addressing). Because the immediate value is negative, the beq instruction branches backwards—four bytes backwards to the instruction that immediately precedes it—to the hout instruction.

Here is the complete program (it is in the file r0204.bin).

r0204.bin

```
0000100 00000 00011 000 00000 0000000 # hout
1111111 00000 00000 000 11101 1100011 # beq: cmp x0 with x0, br if eq
```

Run this program yourself. If you enter

```
rv r0204.bin
```

the load point defaults to 0. The gp register is set to the load point. Thus, the gp register will contain 0. Because the program repeatedly displays the contents of the gp register is hex, it will fill the screen with zeros. But if you run the program by entering

```
rv 0204.bin -L a4
```

the load point is a4 hex. Thus, the gp register is set to a4. With this load point, the program will fill the screen with multiple occurrences of "a4".

Load Upper Immediate and Add Upper Immediate pc Instructions

The lui (load upper immediate) instruction contains a 20-bit immediate value in positions 31 to 12. When executed it loads a copy of itself with its rightmost 12 bits zeroed out into the register specified by its *rd* field. Thus, the effect is to load its immediate value into the upper 20 bits of the specified register and zero out the lower 12 bits. For example, if the immediate value in the instruction is 12345 hex, then the register specified by its *rd* field is loaded with 12345000 hex. Here is its format:

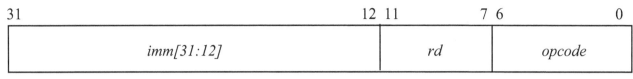

U-type format

After using a `lui` instruction to initialize the upper 20 bits of a register, we can use an `addi` instruction to initialize the lower 12 bits of the register. Thus, with a `lui-addi` sequence of instructions, we can load any 32-bit constant into a register. For example, here is a program that initializes `t0` with the constant 00010010001101000101011001111000 (12345678 hex) using a `lui-addi` sequence, and then displays `t0` in hex. The `lui` instruction loads `t0` with 12345000 hex. The `addi` instruction adds 678 hex to `t0`.

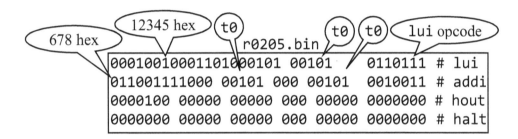

The `auipc` (add upper immediate `pc`) instruction uses the same format as the `lui` instruction. It works the same way as the `lui` instruction except that it also adds the address in the `pc` register (the address at the time the `auipc` instruction is fetched) to the register specified by the *rd* field. That is, it adds the address in the `pc` register before the `pc` register is incremented by 4.

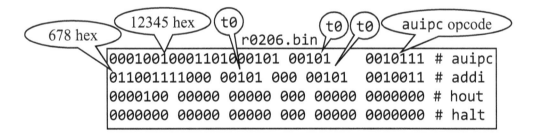

Try running the two programs above, first with no load point (in which case it defaults to 0) and then with a load point of 4. When the load point is 0, then the `pc` register will contain 0 when the `auipc` instruction in `r0206.bin` is fetched. Thus, it loads `t0` with 12345000 + 0 = 12345000 hex. It has the same effect as the `lui` instruction in `r0205.bin`. But when the load point is 4, the `pc` register will contain 4 when the `auipc` instruction is fetched. Thus, the `auipc` instruction will load `t0` with 12345000 + 4 = 12345004. Then when the `addi` instruction adds 678, the result is 12345004 + 678 = 1234567c hex.

There is a complication with both the `lui-addi` sequence and the `auipc-addi` sequence having to do with the sign extension of the immediate value in the `addi` instruction. We will defer discussing this complication for now (see problem 11 in this chapter and the discussion on the `li` and `la` pseudoinstructions in chapter 4).

Jump and Link and Jump and Link Register Instructions

Jump instructions, like the branch instructions, cause a transfer control. But unlike the branch instructions, the jump instructions transfer control *unconditionally*—that is, the jump to a new location *always* occur. The branch instructions conditionally transfer control. They transfer control only if some condition holds. For example, the beq instruction branches only if the contents of the two specified registers are equal. In RISC-V nomenclature, "branch" refers to a conditional transfer of control; "jump" refers to an unconditional transfer of control.

The jump instructions differ from the branch instruction in one more respect: They load the address of the instruction just above it in memory into the register specified by the *rd* field. For example, suppose a jump instruction is at the address 100 hex in memory, and its *rd* field specifies the ra register (x1). When executed, the jump instruction loads the ra register with 104—the address of the next instruction, and it loads the pc register with the jump-to address.

Jump instructions are used to *call* (i.e., transfer control to) subroutines. A subroutine is simply a sequence of instructions that performs some task. For example, a program might need to compute a square root in several places. Rather than repeating the square root code at each place a square root is needed, we can simply place at each of these places a jump instruction that calls a subroutine that computes the square root. After the subroutine computes the requested square root, it has to transfer control back to where it was called from—specifically, to the location in memory right after the jump instruction. We call the address of this location the *return address*. But how does the subroutine know the return address? It is in the register specified by the *rd* in the jump instruction. Thus, the subroutine simply returns control to the address in that register.

By convention, a jump instruction that calls a subroutine specifies the ra register in its *rd* field. Thus, when executed, the jump instruction loads the ra register with the return address ("ra" stands for "return address"). When the subroutine needs to transfer control back to its caller, it simply jumps to the address in the ra register.

Let's refer to the jump instruction that calls a subroutine the "*calling jump instruction*", and the jump instruction in the subroutine that returns control the "*returning jump instruction*". Unlike the calling jump instruction, the returning jump instruction specifies x0 in its *rd* field. This makes sense because a return jump instruction's only effect should be to return control, not to load the register specified by its *rd* field with a return address (recall x0 is permanently set to 0 so it is unaffected by the returning jump instruction).

The mechanism by which a jump instruction transfers control is the same mechanism the branch instructions use. It simply loads the jump-to address into the pc register. Then on the next fetch operation, the CPU will fetch the instruction at the address.

The following diagram shows the flow of control when a subroutine is called:

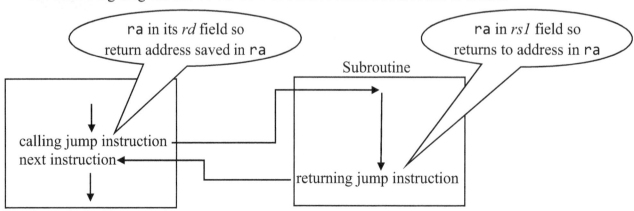

The are two types of the jump instructions: `jal` (jump and link) and `jalr` (jump and link register). The word "link" in the names of both types of instructions indicates that the instructions are used to "link" code that calls a subroutine with that subroutine. Let's investigate the `jal` instruction first.

The `jal` instruction uses `pc`-relative addressing. The jump-to address is given by the contents of the `pc` register at the time the CPU fetches the instruction plus a 21-bit offset, which is in the 20-bit immediate field of the instruction (bit 0 of the offset is not stored because it is always 0). It uses the J-type format:

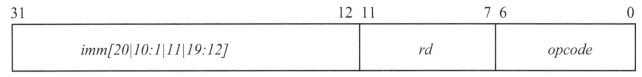

J-type format

Notice in the J-type format, the immediate field holds bits 20 to 1 of the offset but not bit 0. As with the B-type format, the sign bit (bit 20) of the immediate value is in position 31 in the instruction. Bits 10 to 1 are in the same positions in the instruction as the corresponding bits in the I-type instructions. Bits 19 to 12 are in the same positions in the instruction as the corresponding bits in the U-type instructions. As in the branch instructions, the offset is stored in the immediate field in a strange permuted form so that 1) the sign bit is in position 31 of the instruction and 2) for all the instruction formats, corresponding bits in the immediate value fields are in the same position in the instruction to the extent possible.

When executed, the `jal` instruction jumps to the address given by the contents of the `pc` register at the time the `jal` instruction is fetched (which is just the address of the `jal` instruction) plus its 21-bit offset (which is its 20-bit immediate value with 0 added to its right end). It also loads the register specified by its *rd* field with the contents of the `pc` register, *after* the CPU has incremented it by 4—thus, it gets the return address.

The `jalr` instruction uses the I-type format. The jump-to address is given by the contents of the register specified by the *rs1* field plus its immediate value. Like the `jal` instruction, the `jalr` instruction loads the return address into the register specified by its *rd* field.

Both the `jal` and `jalr` instructions can be used as a calling jump instruction. The one to use in any given situation depends on the jump-to address. If the jump-to address is available in a register, then use a `jalr` instruction whose *rs1* field specifies that register. If, on the other hand, the jump-to address is an offset from the calling instruction's location, then use a `jal` instruction whose immediate value provides the offset.

The immediate value in a `jal` instruction represents a 21-bit signed number whose rightmost bit is 0. Thus, its jumping range is 2^{20} bytes backwards and $2^{20} - 2$ bytes forwards (-2 because the rightmost bit of the immediate value is 0). The value 2^{20} is approximately 1 million so the jumping range of a `jal` instruction is considerable. Our `rv` program supports only 64K bytes of memory. So on our simulated RISC-V computer, we never have to worry about exceeding the jumping range of the `jal` instruction.

Because the jump-to address in a `jalr` instruction is provided by a 32-bit register, its jump-to address can be any 32-bit address.

Both the `jal` and `jalr` instruction can serve as calling instructions. However, only the `jalr` instruction can serve as the returning instruction. When a jump instruction calls a subroutine, it loads the return address in a register—by convention, the `ra` register. The returning instruction must return to the address in the `ra` register. A `jalr` instruction can do this, but not a `jal` instruction. To return to its caller, a subroutine uses a `jalr` instruction whose *rs1* field is `ra` and whose immediate value is 0. Thus, it returns to the return address in the `ra` register. Its *rd* field should specify `x0` (the register that permanently contains 0). That way, it simply returns to the caller—it does not also load a return address into a register.

Let's write a program that consists of four instructions:

1. `jal` instruction that calls the subroutine that starts with the `hout` instruction ⏋
2. `halt` ◄———┐ │
3. `hout` instruction that displays `gp` ◄————————————————————————————┘ │
4. `jalr` instruction that returns to the caller (to the `halt` instruction) ⏌

The offset from the `jal` instruction to the start of the subroutine (the `hout` instruction) is 8 bytes. Thus, the 21-bit offset is

20	19										12	11	10									1	0	Bit position
0	0	0	0	0	0	0	0	0	0	0	0	0	0	0	0	0	0	1	0	0	0			Offset

Bits 20 to 1 (the rightmost bit is not stored because it is always 0) are stored in the immediate field of the `jal` instruction in this format: [20|10:1|11|19:12]. Thus, they appear in the `jal` instruction as

```
20     10:1      11    19:12
0   0000000100    0   00000000
```

These bits in the `jal` instruction are followed on the right by the *rd* field that specifies the `ra` register (00001) and the opcode for the `jal` instruction (1101111). Thus, the complete `jal` instruction is

```
imm[20]   imm[10:1]   imm[11]   imm[19:12]   rd      opcode
  0       0000000100      0       00000000   00001   1101111
```

The *rd* field is 00001, the number of the `ra` register. Thus, when executed, this instruction stores the return address into `ra`.

Here is the returning `jalr` instruction:

```
    imm[11:0]        rs1    funct3    rd     opcode
000000000000        00001    000    00000   1100111
```

The *rs1* field is 00001, the number of the `ra` register. The immediate value is 0. Thus, when executed, this instruction returns to the address in the `ra` register (which is the address of the `halt` instruction).

The complete program is in `r0207.bin`:

```
                          r0207.bin
0 0000000100 0 00000000 00001 1101111    # jal
0000000 00000 00000 000 00000 0000000    # halt
0000100 00000 00011 000 00000 0000000    # hout
000000000000 00001 000 00000 1100111     # jalr
```

Because this program displays the contents of the **gp** register (which is initialized with the load point), the program displays the load point. Try running the program with different load points. To specify a load point, use the `-L` argument followed by the load point on the command line when invoking the `rv` program.

Decimal In, Hex In and Newline Instructions

The `rv` program supports input instructions as well as output instructions. For example, the `din` (decimal in) instruction reads a decimal number from the keyboard and loads the corresponding 32-bit binary number into the specified register. Similarly, `hin` (hex in) reads a hex number from the keyboard and loads the corresponding 32-bit binary number into the specified register. All the I/O instructions use the R-type format. The output instructions (like `dout` and `hout`) use the *rs1* field to specify the register that provides the number to be outputted. The input instructions that read a value from the keyboard into a register (like `din` and `hin`) use the *rd* field to specify the register to receive the number that is inputted. Here is a three-instruction program—a `hin`, `dout`, `halt` sequence—that reads a hex number from the keyboard into `t0` (`x5`) and displays its value in decimal.

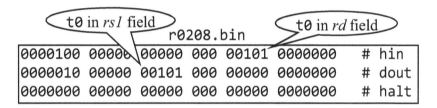

When the `hin` instruction in the program above is executed, the computer will pause, waiting for your input. The program does not give any indication that is waiting for input. So be sure to enter a hex number right after you start the program. If you run this program and enter the hex number 1a, this is what you will see on the display screen:

```
1a
26
```

A better version of this program would prompt the user for the input and label the output. The display would then look like this:

```
Enter hex number
1a
Number in decimal = 26
```

We will learn how to prompt the user and label output in the next chapter.

We often want to a program to move the cursor on the display monitor to the beginning of the next line so output appears on successive lines rather than all on one line. This operation is performed by the `nl` (newline) instruction. For example, if a program has two successive `dout` instructions, their output will appear on the same line with no intervening spaces. However, if we insert a `nl` instruction in between the two `dout` instructions, then the output from the two `dout` instructions will appear on successive lines.

The `nl` instruction, like the other output instructions, uses the R-type format. Its *funct7* field contains 0000001; its *funct3* and opcode fields contain all 0's. Its three register fields (*rs2*, *rs1*, and *rd*) are not used. Here is the `nl` instruction in binary (note it contains only a single 1 bit):

```
   funct7    rs2   rs1   funct3   rd    opcode
  0000001  00000 00000   000    00000  0000000
```

Let's determine the structure of a program that displays the number 100 down to 1, each on a separate line. One approach is to use 100 dout instructions, each displaying one number. A better approach, however, is to use a single dout instruction inside a loop that iterates 100 times. Here is the structure of such a program:

1. Load 100 into t0 with an addi instruction.
2. Display the contents of t0 with a dout instruction. ◄─────────────────────────┐
3. Move cursor to next line with a nl instruction.   │
4. Add −1 to t0 with an addi instruction.   │
5. Conditionally branch to the dout instruction with a bne instruction that compares x0 and t0. ┘
6. halt instruction.

Each time through the loop, the number is t0 in decremented by 1. Thus, the loop displays, 100, 99, 98, and so on. When the number in t0 is 1, it is displayed in step 2, and the number in t0 is then decremented to 0 in step 4, at which point the contents of t0 and x0 (which permanently contains 0) are equal. Thus, the conditional branch in step 5 does not occur because the tested condition (x0 and t0 not equal) is no longer true. Instead, step 6 is executed, terminating the program. Thus, the loop stops displaying numbers after it displays 1.

When writing machine language programs for the RISC-V, you will surely want to have access to a reference that provides format and opcode information for each instruction. Such a reference is in Appendix B and in the file riscvref.pdf. You will find it helpful to print out a copy of riscvref.pdf and have it handy as you write your programs.

Problems

1) Write and run a machine language program in binary that adds 1, 200, and 500 and displays the sum in decimal and hex.

2) Write and run a machine language program that adds −1, −200, and −500 and displays the sum in decimal and hex.

3) Write and run a machine language program that reads in a decimal number (use din). Output the number read in with dout, udout, and hout. udout (unsigned decimal out) works like dout except that it treats the number in the specified register as an unsigned number (dout treats the number as a signed number). Display each number on a separate line. Test your program with −1 and 15.

4) Write and run a machine language program that displays the numbers 100 to 1, each on a separate line. Use a loop.

5) Write and run a machine language program that reads in a positive decimal number and then displays it that number of times.

6) Write and run a machine language program the computes and displays the sum of the first 15 positive odd numbers.

7) Why do the output instructions use the *rs1* field but the input instructions use the *rd* field?

8) An unconditional transfer of control can be provided by either a jal instruction or a beq instruction

whose *rs1* and *rs2* both specify x0. Is there any advantage in using the jal instruction compared with the beq instruction?

9) There is no subtract immediate instruction in the RISC-V instruction set. Why?

10) There is no bgt instruction in the RISC-V instruction set. Why?

11) Write a program that loads t0 with 80000001 hex and t1 with 12345fff hex, and then displays the two registers in hex. Use a lui-addi sequence to load each number. Are you encountering an unanticipated difficulty loading 12345fff?

12) Same as problem 11, but use lw instructions.

13) What is the most positive number that can be loaded into a register with an addi instruction? What is the most negative number?

14) Why do the lw and sw instructions have different formats? Why do the jump instructions not use the U-type format?

15) Is the *funct3* field in the input and output instructions ignored, or does it have to be set to all 0's?

16) Write and run a machine language program that reads in two numbers and displays the larger.

17) Write and run a machine language program that reads in a number and displays 7 times its value. Do NOT do this by summing seven occurrences of the number. *Hint*: First, get twice the number and four times the number.

18) Write and run a machine language program that reads in a decimal number and displays its negation. For example, if it inputs 5, it outputs −5.

19) Write and run a machine language program that reads in a hex number, flips all the bits in its binary representation, and then displays the flipped version in hex.

20) Write and run a machine language program that reads in a number into t0, moves (i.e., copies) the number to t1, and then displays the number in t1. Use the addi instruction to do the move.

3 Assembly Language Part 1

Introduction

Assembly language is a symbolic form of machine language. An assembly language instruction consists of symbols that represent the binary fields of a machine language instruction. Because it is symbolic, assembly language is much easier to read, write, modify, and debug.

Below is a machine language program (in r0301.bin) identical to the machine language program in in r0201.bin from chapter 2 (it loads 2 into t0, loads 3 into t1, adds, puts the sum into t0, and displays the sum in t0). Following the machine language program is the equivalent assembly language program (in r0301.a).

```
                         r0301.bin
1 | 000000010100 00011 010 00101 0000011     # lw
2 | 000000011000 00011 010 00110 0000011     # lw
3 | 0000000 00110 00101 000 00101 0110011     # add
4 | 0000010 00000 00101 000 00000 0000000     # dout
5 | 0000000 00000 00000 000 00000 0000000     # halt
6 | 00000000000000000000000000000010          # data (2)
7 | 00000000000000000000000000000011          # data (3)
```

```
                       r0301.a
1 |           lw t0, x          # load 2 into t0
2 |           lw t1, y          # load 3 into t1
3 |           add t0, t0, t1    # add t0 and t1
4 |           dout t0           # display sum in t0
5 |           halt
6 | x:        .word 2           # word containing 2
7 | y:        .word 3           # word containing 3
```

Note that "#" starts a comment in an assembly language program as well as in a ".bin" file.

Rule: Files containing an assembly language program should have the file name extension ".a":

Consider the first instruction—the lw instruction—in the two programs above. The assembly language program uses "lw" in place of 010 in the *funct3* field and 0000011 in the *opcode* field. We call the names like lw that we use in place of the bits in the machine instruction that specify the operation *mnemonics* because they are easy to remember ("mnemonic" means "aiding memory"). In place of the bits in the machine language instruction that specify the address of the word to load, the assembly language program uses the label x. Think of x as a symbolic address. It represents the address of the line in the program that starts with the label x (line 6). Similarly, in the second instruction, in place of the bits in the machine instruction that specify the address of the word to load, the assembly language program uses the label y. It represents the address of the line that starts with y (line 7).

Line 6 in the assembly language program,

x: .word 2

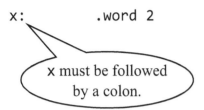

x must be followed
by a colon.

indicates that a word containing 2 in binary should occupy this position in the program. That is, the corresponding word in the machine language program should contain the 32-bit number

00000000000000000000000000000010.

We do not call ".word" a mnemonic because it does not represent the operation in an instruction. Instead, we call it a *directive* because it directs us to do something when translating the program—namely, to replace the line with the specified item (for example, the number 2 in line 6) converted to binary.

Rule: Mnemonics and directives are *case insensitive*, but labels are not. That is, the case of mnemonics and directives does not matter in an assembly language program. Thus, the mnemonics lw, Lw, and LW are equivalent, and so are the directives .word, .Word, and .WORD, but the labels x and X are not.

Rule: A label that *starts* a line must be followed by a colon. For example, the label x on line 6 in r0301.a must be followed by a colon (but not the label x in the lw instruction on line 1).

Rule: A label must start with "_", "$", "@", or a letter. After the first character, the digits 0 to 9 are also allowed. For example, count, a1, @2, $$$, and x_2 are acceptable labels, but 2x, x(4), and y2.2 are not.

Rule: To specify a hex constant in an assembly language program, precede the hex number with "0x" (for example, 0x1a5). To specify a binary constant, prefix the binary number with "0b" (for example, 0b1011). Numbers without a prefix (for example, 123) are treated by the assembler as decimal numbers.

Warning: Most assemblers do not allow constants to be specified in binary.

In a .word directive, we can specify a number in decimal or hex, a character constant (i.e., a character within single quotes), or a label. A character constant is translated to a numeric code that represents that character. For example, 'A', 'B', and 'C' are translated to the binary equivalents of decimal 65, 66, and 67, respectively. The particular coding scheme we use for characters (which most computers use) is *ASCII* (American Standard Code for Information Interchange). A label in a .word directive is translated to its corresponding 32-bit address. For example, suppose the following statements appear in a program, and the address of a is 124 hex (that is, the address of the line that starts with the label a is 124 hex):

```
                 Assume this word is at the address 124
a:        .word 3     # translated to the binary equivalent of 3 decimal
b:        .word 0x1a5 # translated to the binary equivalent of 1a5 hex
c:        .word 'A'   # translated to the binary equivalent of 65 decimal
d:        .word a     # translated to the binary equivalent of 124 hex
```

Then the word in memory corresponding to the line that starts with the label d would contain the address of **a**. Thus, it would contain124 hex

Rule: A character constant should be specified with the character enclosed in *single* quotes. Right: `'A'`. Wrong: `"A"`.

A `.word` directive can specify a sequence of constants or labels separated by commas. Such a sequence is translated to consecutive words in memory. For example,

```
a:        .word 3, 0x1a5, 'A', a
```

is translated to four words that respectively contain 3, 0x1a5, the ASCII code for `'A'`, and the address of a. Thus, this one `.word` directive is equivalent to the preceding four `.word` directives, but without the labels b, c and d.

One of the great benefits of using labels in place of addresses is that insertions and deletions do not require any changes in labels. For example, suppose we want the modify the program in `r0301.a` so that it displays the computed sum in both decimal and hex. In the assembly language program, we simply insert

```
        nl          ; move cursor to next line
        hout t0     ; displays value in t0 in hex
```

just before the `halt` instruction, and re-assemble. The `nl` (newline) instruction moves the cursor to the beginning of the next line; the `hout` instruction displays the contents of the specified register in hex. *No other changes are required.* But in the machine language program in `r0301.bin`, the insertion of the machine language instructions `nl` and `hout` *changes the addresses of the two data words* at the bottom of the program. Thus, the addresses in the two `lw` instructions have to be adjusted so that they correspond to the new addresses of the data. In a large program with many instructions that address data, a *single insertion or deletion might require hundreds of additional modifications* to correct for the altered addresses of the data. Clearly, this would be a clerical nightmare.

Assembly language, of course, is not machine language. It cannot be executed directly by the CPU. Before an assembly language program can be executed, it must be translated to machine language. It is tedious but not difficult to translate assembly language programs to machine language by hand. But an easier and more reliable approach is to use a program—called an *assembler*—to do the translation for us. The `rv` program that we have been using to run machine language programs is also an assembler. To assemble and execute the program in `r0301.a`, enter on the command line

```
    rv r0301.a        (on Windows)
```
or
```
    ./rv r0301.a      (on OS X, Linux, or Raspbian)
```

Note: From this point on, we will illustrate the command line commands with only the Windows alternative. Be sure to remember to prefix commands on the command line with "./" if you are using Mac OS X, Linux, or Raspbian. Alternatively, on Mac OS X, Linux, and Raspbian, you can change the PATH variable so it includes the current directory (see `rv.txt` on how to do this). Then the "./" prefix is not required.

The assembly process consists of two passes over the program in the input file. During the second pass over the assembly language program in `r0301.a`, the assembler outputs the machine code to the file `r0301.e`. This file has the extension ".e" (which indicates the file holds an executable machine language program) and the same base name as the input file. After assembling the source program, the `rv` program then executes the program in the executable file it creates. You will see on the display screen

```
rv Version 3.4 Copyright (c) 2019 by Anthony J. Dos Reis
5
```

The `rv` program also produces ".lst" and ".bst" files with the same base name as the input file. Thus, for the input file `r0301.a`, it produces the files `r0301.lst` and `r0301.bst`. These files contain the *source program* (i.e., the "source" of the assembly process, which is, the assembly language program) along with the corresponding machine code in hex (`r0301.lst`) or in binary (`r0301.bst`). Here is the `r0301.lst` file produced by the `rv` program:

r0301.lst

```
rv Version 3.4                          Mon Jul 15 02:25:45 2019
Anthony J. Dos Reis


Header
R
L 00000000
L 00000004
C


Loc      Code              Source Code
0000    0141a283              lw t0, x        # load 2 into t0
0004    0181a303              lw t1, y        # load 3 into t1
0008    006282b3              add t0, t0, t1  # add t0 and t1
000c    04028000              dout t0         # display sum in t0
0010    00000000              halt
0014    00000002 x:           .word 2         # data (2)
0018    00000003 y:           .word 3         # data(3)
========================================================= Output
5

========================================= Program statistics
Input file name      = r0301.a
Instructions executed = 5 (decimal)
Program size          = 1c (hex) 28 (decimal)
Load point            = 0 (hex) 0 (decimal)
Programmer            = Anthony J. Dos Reis
```

We can optionally include an offset in the second operand of a `lw` instruction. The offset should be separated from the label with a plus or minu sign. If an offset is specified, then the effective address is the address of the label plus or minus the offset. For example, we can replace the second instruction in the `r0301.a` (the instruction that loads from y) with

```
lw t1, x+4   # load 3 into t1
```

It loads from the location corresponding to the x label plus 4 bytes. Thus, it loads from y.

Strings

A string in assembly language is a sequence of characters enclosed in double quotes. Each character in a string is represented by a numeric code in the corresponding machine language. The code that our RISC-V computer uses is ASCII (American Standard Code for Information Interchange). ASCII represents each character with a seven-bit number which is usually zero-extended to 8 bits. Here are the ASCII codes for several characters:

```
'A':   01000001  (41 hex, 65 decimal)
'a':   01100001  (61 hex, 97 decimal)
'B';   01000010  (42 hex, 66 decimal)
'b':   01100010  (62 hex, 98 decimal)
'0':   00110000  (30 hex, 48 decimal)
'1':   00110001  (31 hex, 49 decimal)
' ':   00100000  (20 hex, 32 decimal)
'\t':  00001010  (09 hex, 9 decimal)
'\n':  00001010  (0A hex, 10 decimal)
'\r':  00001101  (0D hex, 13 decimal)
```

The uppercase letters are assigned numbers in ascending order, starting from 41 hex. The lowercase letters are assigned numbers in ascending order, starting from 61 hex. The code for each uppercase letter differs from the code for the lowercase for that letter in only bit 5. In the uppercase letter, bit 5 is 0; in the lowercase letter, bit 5 is 1. For example, consider the letter 'A':

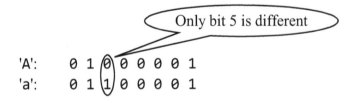

The digits are assigned numbers in ascending order starting from 30 hex. '\t' is the *horizontal tab character*. '\n' is the *newline character*. '\r' is the *return character*. Corresponding to the tab, newline, and return characters, there are no displayable characters. Thus, we have to represent them with an *escape sequence*: a backslash followed by a regular letter. For example, '\n' represents the newline character— not the letter n. On systems other than Windows, just the '\n' character usually marks the end of each line in a text file. On Windows systems, the two-character sequence, '\r', '\n', marks the end of each line of a text file. For example, suppose a text file on a Windows system contains the following text:

```
AB
0 1
```

It is represented with the following sequence of ASCII codes (given in hex):

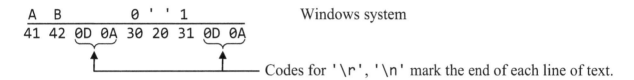

Windows system

Codes for `'\r'`, `'\n'` mark the end of each line of text.

But on a Mac OS X, Linux, or Raspbian system, the two lines of text are represented with

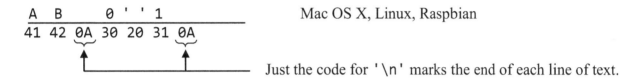

Mac OS X, Linux, Raspbian

Just the code for `'\n'` marks the end of each line of text.

The newline, return, tab, and space characters are called *whitespace* because they do not produce a displayable character on a printed paper. You see just the white background of the paper—hence the name "whitespace."

A string of characters in an assembly language program is represented by the sequence of their ASCII codes, each occupying *one byte*, followed by the *null character* (the character represented by all zero bits). For example, if the string "AB" is in memory starting at location 200, the locations of memory starting at the address 200 contain the following codes (shown in hex):

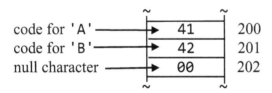

The null character marks the end of the string.

It is a good idea to memorize the ASCII codes for `'A'`, `'a'`, `'0'`, space, `'\n'`, and `'\r'`. That will allow you to quickly identify and decipher strings in their binary or hex representations.

To display a string on the display monitor, we use the **sout** (string out) I/O instruction. It has the same format as the **dout** and **hout** instructions. When a **sout** instruction is executed, the specified register should contain the address of the first character of the string. The **sout** instruction displays all the characters in memory starting from that address up to the null character at the end of the string.

Let's write a program that displays the string "hello\n". To define this string in our program we use the **.asciz** directive. When the assembler translates a line with the **.asciz** directive, it places the codes for the characters that make up the string into successive bytes, and terminates the string with the null character. The "z" in ".asciz" is an indication that the string is terminated with a byte than contains zero (i.e., the null character). Here is the program:

```
                              r0302.a
1               lw t0, as      # load address of string into t0
2               sout t0        # display string whose address is in t0
3               halt
4  s:           .asciz "hello\n"
5  as:          .word s        # address of string
```

Note: The .string directive is equivalent to the .asciz directive. Use whichever you prefer.

The assembler translates the .word directive at the bottom of the program to the address of s. Thus, the lw instruction on line 1 loads the address of s into t0. The sout instruction then displays the string whose address is in t0. The '\n' at the end of the string moves the cursor to the beginning of the next line. Thus, if the sout instruction were followed by another output instruction, that instruction would output on the line that follows the "hello\n" line.

To input a string from the keyboard into memory, we use the sin (string in) instruction. When executed, the specified register should have the address of the input buffer (i.e., the block of memory that is to receive the inputted string). To reserve a block of memory as an input buffer, we use the .zero directive. For example, the following directive reserves and initializes to zero 100 bytes of memory:

```
buf:        .zero 100   # reserves and zeros out 100 bytes of memory
```

Note: Like the .zero directive, the .space directive reserves and initializes the specified number of bytes of memory. But in a .space directive, a second operand is specified whose value is used to initialize each byte in the reserved block. For example,

```
buf:        .space 100, 5
```

initializes each byte of the 100-byte block to 5.

Let's try out the sin instruction. Using it, let's read in a string. Then using sout, let's echo that string to the display. Before inputting a string, the program prompts the user for the string. Here is the program:

```
                             r0303.a
1               lw t0, aprompt # load t0 with address of prompt message
2               sout t0        # prompt user for string
3               lw t0, abuf    # load t0 with the address of the buffer
4               sin t0         # input string into buffer
5               sout t0        # echo string to the display
6               halt
7  aprompt: .word prompt    # address of prompt string
8  prompt:   .asciz "Enter string\n"
9  abuf:     .word buf       # address of the input buffer
10 buf:      .zero 100       # 100-byte input buffer
```

When the sin instruction on line 4 in the program above is executed, it does not affect the address in t0.

Thus, when the subsequent `sout` instruction is executed, `t0` still contains the address of the beginning of the input buffer (which now contains the inputted string). Thus, the `sout` instruction outputs the string just inputted.

Suppose you enter the string "goodbye" when you run the program above with `rv`. You will see on the screen

```
Enter string ←— prompt message
goodbye        ←— inputted string
goodbye        ←— echoed string
```

Hitting the Enter key at the end of inputting a string causes the cursor to move to the beginning of the next line. Thus, the inputted string and the echoed string appear on successive lines. However, when outputting a string, the cursor does not automatically move to the next line. To move the cursor to the next line, include a newline character ('\n') at the end of the outputted string (as we did in the prompt message in `r0303.a`) or insert a `nl` instruction in your program after the `sout` instruction.

The `sin` instruction uses its *rs1* field to specify the register used in the input operation. For example, *rs1* field in the `sin` instruction in `r0303.a` contains 00101, the number of the `t0` register (recall `t0` is `x5`). But all the other input instructions (like `din` and `hin`) use the *rd* field—not the *rs1* field—to specify the register used in the input operation. This inconsistency makes sense. In the input instructions like `din` and `hin`, the specified register receives the inputted value. It is the destination of the inputted value. Thus, it is specified by the *rd* field in the instruction (recall that "rd" stands for "register destination"). But in the `sin` instruction, the specified register does not receive the inputted string—memory does.

Text and Binary Files

There are basically two kinds of computer files: text and binary. All computer files store information in the form of a sequence of 1's and 0's. But in text files, each byte (i.e, 8-bit group) of the file represents a single character. For example, in a text file, a byte equal to 00110010 represents the character "2". We call such files *text files* to distinguish them from *binary files*, which are files whose individual bytes do not represent characters. Assembly language source programs and the ".bin" and ".hex" files we used in chapter 2 are examples of text files. For example, the instruction on the first line of the `r0201.bin` file is

```
000000010100 00011 010 00101 0000011    # lw
```

Each character in this line—each `0`, each `1`, each space, #, l, and w—is represented by an 8-bit ASCII code. For example, each 0 is represented with the 8-bit code 00110000 (30 hex); each 1 is represented with 00110001 (31 hex), and each space is represented with 00100000 (20 hex). This line contains a total of 45 characters, each requiring 8 bits. Thus, in `r0201.bin`, the line is represented by a sequence of 45 × 8 bits = 360 bits. The line represents a machine instruction, but it is *not* a machine instruction. A machine instruction consists of a sequence of 32 bits—*not* 360 bits. Thus, before the `rv` program can execute the program in `r0201.bin`, it has to convert each instruction to a 32-bit machine instruction. For example, it has to convert the first line consisting of 360 bits into these 32 bits:

```
00000001010000011010001010000011
```

The ".e" file that rv creates when it inputs r0201.bin contains the converted form of the program. For example, when you run r0201.bin by entering

```
    rv r0201.bin
```

rv creates the file r0201.e (as well as r0201.lst and r0201.bst). We call r0201.e an *executable file* because it is ready to be executed. If we want to run the program again, we can bypass the conversion step by inputting r0201.e instead of r0201.bin:

```
    rv r0201.e
```

We can also do this with assembly language programs. That is, after assembling and running a program, we can run the program again with rv by specifying on the command line the ".e" file the assembler created on the first run, thereby bypassing a second conversion of assembly code to machine code.

ASCII In and ASCII Out instructions

The ain (ASCII in) instruction inputs a character from the keyboard into the specified register. The aout (ASCII out) instruction outputs the character in the specified register to the display. For example, the following program inputs a character from the keyboard with the ain instruction, then displays it using the aout, dout, and hout instruction:

r0304.a

```
1           lw t0, aprompt  # load t0 with address of prompt message
2           sout t0         # prompt user to enter character
3           ain t0          # input a character
4           aout t0         # echo the character
5           nl              # move cursor to next line
6           dout t0         # output code for character in decimal
7           nl              # move cursor to next line
8           hout t0         # output code for character in hex
9           halt
10 prompt:  .asciz "Enter character: "
11 aprompt: .word prompt
```

The ain instruction in r0304.a inputs a character into the t0 register (in response to the ain instruction, be sure to input the character *without* the quotes). What is actually inputted is the ASCII code for the character that is entered on the keyboard. For example, if the character A is entered in response to the ain instruction, then the ASCII code for A, which is 01000001 (41 hex, 65 decimal) zero extended to 32 bits is loaded into t0 by the instruction. The aout instruction then takes this code and outputs the corresponding character (so it outputs A). The dout instruction outputs the code in decimal (so it outputs 65). The hout instruction outputs the code in hex (so it outputs 41). The nl (newline) instructions move the cursor to the next line so each output appears on a separate line. We do not need a nl instruction after the `ain` instruction because the Enter key you hit after entering a character moves the cursor to the next line. Here is what the display will look like if you input A:

```
Enter character: A
A
65
41
```

Within an assembly language program, character constants must be enclosed single quotes. For example, to initialize `t0` with 'A', we can use the following `addi` instruction:

```
        addi t0, x0, 'A'
```

The assembler translates the character constant to its ASCII code, and inserts it into the immediate field of `addi` instruction. When the instruction is executed, it adds the contents of `x0` (which is 0) and the ASCII code of the character in its immediate field. It then loads the sum (which is just the ASCII code for the character) into `t0`. However, in response to an `ain` instruction, you should *not* enclose the character in quotes. Similarly, when entering a string in response to the `sin` instruction, you should *not* enclose the string in quotes (unless you want the quotes to be included in the inputted string).

Rule: In an assembly language program, strings are enclosed in double quotes; character constants are enclosed in single quotes.

Loops in Assembly Language and the .equ Directive

Loops are easy to write in assembly language. We simply use a branch instruction that specifies the branch-to addresses with a label (we will see later, we also can use jump instructions to create loops). Let's write a program that uses a loop to compute the square of any positive integer. It computes squares using the following property of squares:

(sum of the first n positive odd integers) = n^2

 For example, the sum of the first 3 odd integers is equal to 3^2: $1 + 3 + 5 = 9 = 3^2$. Thus, to computer n^2, we simply sum up the first n odd integers using a loop that executes n times. In our program, we use `t0` to hold the current odd number. `t0` is initialized to 1. Each time through the loop, `t0` is incremented by 2. Thus, the first time through the loop, it holds the first odd number (1); the second time through the loop, it holds the second odd number (3), and so on. `t1` functions as an *accumulator*: It "accumulates" the sum. It is initialized to 0. Each time through the loop, `t0` (the current odd number) is added to `t1`. The program prompts the user for n (the number to be squared), and reads it into `t2`. It then copies `t2` to `t3`. `t3` functions as the *loop counter*. That is, it keeps track of the number of times the loop has executed (by counting down from n to 0). When `t3` reaches 0, the exit from the loop occurs. `t1` at that point will have the sum of the first n odd integers, which is the square of n. Following the loop is a `dout` instruction that displays the square in `t1`. Here is the program:

r0305.a

```
 1 # This program reads in a positive integer n and computes its
 2 # square by adding the first n positive odd integers
 3 # t0 current odd number
 4 # t1 accumulator that accumulates the sum
 5 # t2 n (the number to be squared
 6 # t3 loop counter
 7
 8           addi t0, x0, 1      # init current odd number to 1
 9           addi t1, x0, 0      # init accumulator to 0
10           lw t4, aprompt      # get address of prompt message
11           sout t4             # prompt user for n
12           din t2              # input n
13           addi t3, t2, 0      # initialize loop counter with n
14
15 loop:     add  t1, t1, t0     # add current odd number in t0 to t1
16           addi t0, t0, 2      # increase t0 to next odd number
17           addi t3, t3, -1     # decrement loop counter in t3
18           bne t3, x0, loop    # branch if loop counter not 0
19
20           lw t4, amsg1        # get address of msg1
21           sout t4             # output "Square of "
22           dout t2             # output n
23           lw t4, amsg2        # get address of msg2
24           sout t4             # output " = "
25           dout t1             # output the square
26           halt                # terminate program
27
28 aprompt:  .word prompt
29 prompt:   .asciz "Enter positive integer: "
30 amsg1:    .word msg1
31 msg1:     .asciz "Square of "
32 amsg2:    .word msg2
33 msg2:     .asciz " = "
```

The program in r0305.a nicely illustrates the versatility of the addi instruction. On line 8, it initializes t0 to 1 (the first odd number). On line 13, it moves (i.e., copies) *n* in t2 into the loop counter t3. On line 16, it adds 2 to t0 (to get the next odd number). On line 17 is subtracts 1 (by adding −1) from the loop counter in t3. Note that the immediate field in an addi instructions holds a 12-bit signed number, giving it a range limited to −2048 to +2047. Thus, a single addi instruction cannot initialize a register with a number outside that range, or add a number to a register outside that range.

To make the program in r0305.a more readable, we

- included a prolog that describes what the program does and indicates what values the t0, t1, t2, and t3 registers hold.
- commented every instruction.
- used blank lines to separate the program into logical parts.

Nevertheless, the program is still somewhat difficult to follow, principally because the names of the registers do not reflect the values they hold. Thus, as we read the program, we have to remember that t0 is the current odd number, t1 is the accumulator, and so on. However, using .equ directives, we can give the registers meaningful names and then use those names in place of the register names.

An .equ directive has two operands separated by a comma. Wherever the first operand (a name) appears in the program, the assembler replaces it with the second operand. Here is the same program as in r0305.a, but with .equ directives for the register names:

r0305x.a

```
 1 | # This program reads in a positive integer n and computes its
 2 | # square by adding the first n positive odd integers
 3 |           .equ odd, t0              # holds current odd number
 4 |           .equ accum, t1            # accumulator for the sum
 5 |           .equ n, t2                # n
 6 |           .equ ctr, t3              # loop counter
 7 |
 8 |           addi odd, x0, 1           # init current odd number to 1
 9 |           addi accum, x0, 0         # init accumulator to 0
10 |           lw t4, aprompt            # get address of prompt message
11 |           sout t4                   # prompt user for n
12 |           din n                     # input n
13 |           addi ctr, n, 0            # initialize counter with n
14 |
15 | loop:     add  accum, accum, odd    # add current odd number to accum
16 |           addi odd, odd, 2          # increase odd to next odd number
17 |           addi ctr, ctr, -1         # decrement loop counter
18 |           bne ctr, x0, loop         # branch if loop counter not 0
19 |
20 |           lw t4, amsg1              # get address of msg1
21 |           sout t4                   # output "Square of "
22 |           dout n                    # output n
23 |           lw t4, amsg2              # get address of msg2
24 |           sout t4                   # output " = "
25 |           dout accum                # output the square in accum
26 |           halt
27 |
28 | aprompt:  .word prompt
29 | prompt:   .asciz "Enter positive integer: "
30 | amsg1:    .word msg1
31 | msg1:     .asciz "Square of "
32 | amsg2:    .word msg2
33 | msg2:     .asciz " = "
```

With meaningful names in place of the register names, the logic of the program is considerably easier to follow.

Another use of .equ directives is to give meaningful names to numbers. For example, if your program has a loop that executes 365 times, once for each day of the year, you can use `days_in_year` in place of 365 in your program if you include the following directive:

```
.equ days_in_year, 365
```

.equ directives should precede any lines of code that use the names they equate. It is customary to put .equ directives at the beginning of the program (as we did in r0305x.a).

Bitwise Operations

A bitwise operation performs an operation on each bit of a number or on each pair of corresponding bits in two numbers. To keep our examples simple, let's illustrate bitwise operations with four-bit numbers. Consider the following two four-bit numbers:

```
1100
0101
0100  ←——— result of bitwise AND operation
 ↑
 └── This bit is 1 because the two bits ANDed in this column are both 1.
```

A bitwise AND of these two numbers ANDs the pair of bits in each column. Thus, the bitwise AND requires four separate AND operations—one for each column. The result bit in each column is 1 if the two bits in that column are 1. Otherwise, the result bit is 0.

The bitwise AND operation is used to test a bit in a number. For example, to test the third bit from the right of the four-bit number, 0101, AND the number with 0100:

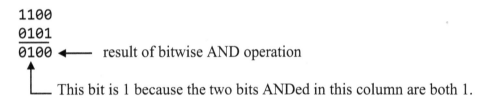

```
0101  tested number
0100  mask
0100  ←——— result of bitwise AND operation
 ↑
 └── This 1 bit indicates that the third bit from the right of the top number is 1.
```

ANDing a bit with 0 produces a 0 bit. ANDing a bit with 1 produces that bit. Thus, the result of the AND operation illustrated above is all 0's except -for the third bit from the right (the one that is the result of ANDing with 1). If the result is nonzero (as it is in this example), then the third bit from the right in the tested number must be 1. If the result is zero, then that bit must be 0. Thus, the result depends *just* on the third bit from the right in the tested number. We call the number that we AND with the tested number a *mask*. The mask in this example "masks" (i.e., hides) all the bits in the tested number (by ANDing them with 0) we do *not* want to test. Thus, the result of the test depends only on the unmasked bit (i.e., on the bit that corresponds to the 1 bit in the mask).

A bitwise AND operation can also be used to zero out a bit. For example, if we AND a four-bit number with 1011, the result is the given number with its third bit from the right set to 0 (because the bit in the given number is ANDed with 0). The other bits are unaffected because they are ANDed with 1.

In a bitwise OR operation, each pair of bits is ORed. The result in each column is 1 if either bit or both bits in that column are 1. If both bits are 0, then the result bit is 0:

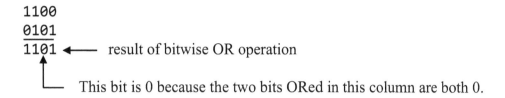

This bit is 0 because the two bits ORed in this column are both 0.

A bitwise OR operation is used to set a bit in a number to 1. For example, if we OR a four-bit number with 0100, the result is the given number with its third bit from the right set to 1 (because the bit in the given number is ORed with 1). The other bits are unaffected because they are ORed with 0.

In a bitwise XOR (exclusive OR) operation, each pair of bits is XORed. The result in each column is 1 if the two bits in that column are different. If both bits are the same, then the result bit is 0:

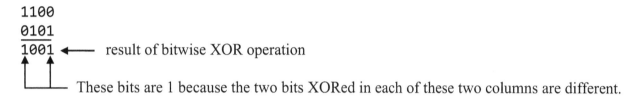

These bits are 1 because the two bits XORed in each of these two columns are different.

A bitwise XOR operation is used to flip a bit in a number. For example, if we XOR a four-bit number with 0100, the result is the given number with its third bit flipped (i.e., 1 becomes 0, and 0 becomes 1). The other bits are unaffected because they are XORed with 0.

Recall that RISC-V has two types of integer add instructions. One (`add`) uses the R-type format and takes three register operands. The other (`addi`) uses the I-type format and takes three operands: two register operands and one immediate value. For each bitwise operation, there is a similar pair of instructions:

- `and, andi`
- `or, ori`
- `xor, xori`

Let's write a program that

- changes a lowercase letter to uppercase (using `andi`),
- changes an uppercase letter to lowercase (using `ori`),
- changes the case of a letter (using `xori`).

Recall that the case of a letter is determined by the bit it position 5 of its ASCII code. If bit 5 is 0, the letter is in uppercase; if bit 5 is 1, the letter is in lowercase. Thus, our program has to modify bit 5 to effect the changes listed above. For example, suppose the ASCII code of a letter in in `t0`. To convert a lowercase letter to uppercase, we set bit 5 to 0 using `andi` and the mask 0xdf (11011111 in binary).

```
andi t0, t0, 0xdf
```

To convert an uppercase letter to lowercase, we set bit 5 to 1 using `ori` and the mask 0x20 (00100000 in binary):

```
ori t0, t0, 0x20
```

To change the case of a letter, we flip bit 5 using xori and the mask 0x20 (00100000 in binary):

```
xori t0, t0, 0x20
```

Here is the program:

```
                                  r0306.a
1         lw t0, aprompt1    # load t0 with address of prompt msg
2         sout t0            # display prompt message
3         ain t0             # read a character into t0
4         andi t0, t0, 0xdf  # change to uppercase
5         aout t0            # display modified character
6         nl                 # move cursor to the next line
7         lw t0, aprompt2    # load t0 with address of prompt msg
8         sout t0            # display prompt message
9         ain t0             # read a character into t0
10        ori t0, t0, 0x20   # change to lowercase
11        aout t0            # display modified character
12        nl                 # move cursor to the next line
13        lw t0, prompt3     # load t0 with the prompt message
14        sout t0            # display prompt message
15        ain t0             # read a character into t0
16        xori t0, t0, 0x20  # change case
17        aout t0            # display modified character
18        halt
19 prompt1:  .asciz "Enter lowercase letter\n"
20 aprompt1: .word prompt1
21 prompt2:  .asciz "Enter uppercase letter\n"
22 aprompt2: .word prompt2
23 prompt3:  .asciz "Enter a letter in either case\n"
24 aprompt3: .word prompt3
```

Another application of the bitwise instructions is to adjust a number to a multiple of a power of 2. For example, suppose we want to adjust the number in t0 so that it is a multiple of 4. If it is not already a multiple of 4, we can either decrease it to the next lower multiple of 4 or increase it to the next higher multiple of 4. A number in binary is a multiple of 4 if and only if its two rightmost bits are 0. Thus, to decrease t0 to the next lower multiple of 4 if it is not already a multiple of 4, we simply zero out its two rightmost bits with an andi instruction:

```
andi t0, t0, 0xfffffffc
```

Note that here we are specifying an 8-digit hex mask because we are masking the 32-bit number in t0. This instruction has no effect if the number in t0 is already a multiple of 4. To increase t0 to the next higher multiple of 4 if it is not already a multiple of 4, we add 3 to increase it so that it is above the next multiple of 4, then zero out its two rightmost bits to set it equal to that multiple of 4:

```
addi t0, t0, 3
andi t0, t0, 0xfffffffc
```

If t0 is already a multiple of 4, this sequence leaves t0 unmodified.

Dereferencing Pointers

The .word directive in the last line of the following program has the label x as its operand:

```
addr                          r0307.a
0000          lw t0, ax       # load t0 with addr of x
0004          lw t1, 0(t0)    # load what t0 is pointing to
0008          dout t1         # display 5 (value from x)
000c          nl              # move cursor to the next line
0010          addi t1, t1, 1  # add 1 to value from x
0014          sw t1, 0(t0)    # store new value into x
0018          lw t1, 4(t0)    # load word after x (y)
001c          dout t1         # displays 7 (value from y)
0020          nl              # move cursor to the next line
0024          lw t1, -4(t0)   # load word preceding x
0028          dout t1         # displays 11
002c          halt
0030          .word 11
0034  x:      .word 5                    Label as operand
0038  y:      .word 7
003c  ax:     .word x         # address of x
```

A label is a symbolic address. Thus, when the assembler translates the last line in r0307.a to binary, it translates it to the binary address of x, which for this program is 0034 hex. Here is a display of the last three lines of the program in memory (the contents of each location are shown in hex):

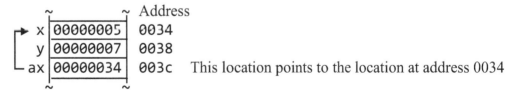

```
              ~            ~   Address
      ┌──► x │00000005│   0034
      │    y │00000007│   0038
      └── ax │00000034│   003c   This location points to the location at address 0034
              ~            ~
```

Because the location corresponding to the label ax has the address of x, we can think of ax as "pointing to" x. If we are not interested in the precise layout of x and ax in memory, we can represent x and ax with the following diagram:

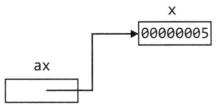

The arrow emanating from ax pointing to x indicates that ax has the address of x. If we use the pointer (i.e., address) in ax to get to what it is pointing to, we say we are *dereferencing* the pointer in ax. In other words, to dereference a pointer means to go to where the pointer is pointing.

We use the load and store instructions, lw and sw, to dereference pointers. In r0307.a, to access x via the pointer in ax, we first load the pointer in ax into t0:

```
lw t0, ax        # load t0 with the address of x
```

We then load what t0 is pointing to into t1:

```
lw t1, 0(t0)     # load t1 with what t0 is pointing to
```

Of course, it would be better to simply load t1 directly from x. But it is often the case that the memory location has no associated label (examples of this are given in the section that follows on stacks). So we cannot access it directly with a label.

Unlike the lw instructions we have already seen, the lw instruction above does not have a label as its second operand. Instead it has a register within parentheses preceded by an offset. The contents of the specified register (t0 in this example) plus the offset (0 in this example) is the address of the memory location from which the lw instruction loads. Because t0 has the address of x and the offset is 0, this instruction loads from the word labeled with x. Now suppose we execute

```
lw t1, 4(t0)     # load from address given by t0 contents + 4
```

with the same value in t0 (the address of x). Now the effective address is the address in t0 plus the offset 4—the address of the word that follows x. Thus, it loads the word that follows the word at x. The offset can be negative. Thus, the instruction

```
lw t1, -4(t0)
```

loads the word that precedes the word at x. The program in r0307.a displays 5, 7, and 11 in that order.

Rule: In assembly language, a register within parentheses provides a *memory address*—the address given by the contents of the parenthesized register plus the offset that precedes the parentheses. In a load instruction, it is the address of the load-from location. In a store instruction, it is the address of the store-to location. In a jalr instruction, it is the jump-to address. For example,

```
lw t1, -4(t0)    # load from (address in t0)-4
sw t1, 8(t0)     # store at (address in t0)+8
jalr x0, 0(ra)   # jump to (address in ra)+0
```

Note: If a load or store instruction has a label as its second operand, it is assembled to a machine instruction that has the number of the gp register in its *rs1* field. If, however, the second operand specifies a register (like the instructions above), then the number of that register goes into the *rs1* field.

Accessing the Stack

A *stack* is a linear data structure that is accessed from one side only. The side accessed is called the *top* of the stack. The operation that adds a word to the top of the stack is called a *push*; the operation that removes the word on top of the stack is called a *pop*.

In an assembly language program, the stack is located at the top of memory (i.e., starting at the word at the address 65532). As words are pushed onto the stack, the stack grows in the downward direction (i.e., toward locations with smaller addresses). Thus, on a push, the address of the top of the stack decreases by 4 (the number of bytes in a word); on a pop, the address increases by 4. To keep track of the top of the stack, we use by convention the sp register (x2). "sp" is for "stack pointer."

To push a word onto the stack, we first decrement the sp register by 4 so that it points to the available space just below the word that is currently on the top of the stack:

```
addi sp, sp, -4
```

We then store the word to be pushed into the location sp points to. For example, to push the word in t0, we use

```
sw t0, 0(sp)      # dereference pointer in sp
```

Note that the location sp points to has no associated label. So to get to it, we *have to* dereference the pointer in sp.

Before a translated assembly language program starts executing, the sp register is initialized by the rv program (acting as the OS) to 10000 hex. Because a push operation first decrements the sp register by 4, the first push stores into location 10000 − 4 = fffc hex = 65532 decimal.

Here are the before and after pictures for a push of 11 (after 25, −9, and 7 have already been pushed):

Before push of 11

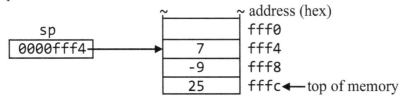

After push of 11

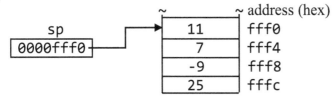

When several items have been pushed onto the stack, we frequently want to access them without popping them. We do this with the lw and sw instructions. To use these instructions, we need a register to point to the area of the stack we want to access. For that purpose, we can use the sp register (x2) or the fp register (x8). Let's first see how the fp register would be used, although, in general, it is better to use the sp register.

We often call the area of the stack we want to access a stack *frame*. Hence, the name "fp" is for "frame pointer." Suppose the stack, sp, fp, and memory are configured as follows:

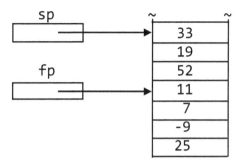

If we then execute the following instruction,

```
lw t0, 8(fp)      # load from address in fp plus 8
```

t0 is loaded from the address given by the contents of fp plus an 8-byte offset. fp is pointing to the location that contains 11 in the diagram above. A positive 8-byte offset (which is two words) from this location is the address of the location that has −9. Thus, this instruction loads t0 with −9.

The offset can be either positive or negative, or zero. For example, the following instruction,

```
lw t0, -12(fp)   # load from address in fp minus 12
```

loads t0 with 33, which is three words (12 bytes) below the location that fp is pointing to.

Using a sw instruction, we can modify a word in the stack frame. For example, if the contents of t0 are 100, then the following instruction stores 100 in the stack frame shown above, overlaying the 7:

```
sw t0, 4(fp)      # store into address fp plus 4
```

Sometimes we want to reserve one or more slots on the stack into which we later can store values. To do that, we simply decrement the value in sp by some multiple of 4 using the addi instruction. For example, to reserve two slots on the stack, we execute

```
addi sp, sp, -8  # reserve two words (8 bytes) on stack
```

This instruction transforms our stack configuration to

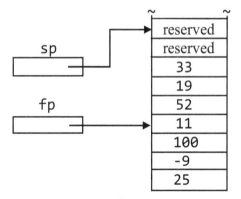

We now have two reserved slots on the stack that we can use later.

Instead of using the `fp` register to access a stack frame, we can also use the `sp` register. For example, to load `t0` from the stack slot that contains 52 (after reserving two slots), we can use

```
        lw t0, 16(sp)       # using sp
```
instead of
```
        lw t0, -4(fp)       # using fp
```

A potential problem with using `sp`, however, it that the offset to a value on the stack changes whenever a push or pop operation occurs. For example, if we push another word onto the stack shown above, then to access the slot that contains 52, we now need the offset 20 because the push operation decrements the address in `sp` by 4. The required `lw` instruction is now

```
        lw t0, 20(sp)       # now need the offset 20 to access -1 on the stack
```

But the `fp` register is not affected by pushes and pops. Thus, the offset to 52 relative to the location `fp` points to remains the same. The required instruction is still

```
        lw t0, -4(fp)       # use same offset as before push
```

The disadvantage of using the `fp` register is that its use requires extra instructions to maintain it with the proper address. It also makes the `fp` register (`x8`) unavailable for other uses. Moreover, we can avoid the problem of changing offsets when we use the `sp` register to access the stack. To do this, we reserve space for the entire stack frame *in advance* with a single `addi` instruction, thereby eliminating the need for subsequent `addi` instructions to allocate space on the stack for push or reserve operations. We can then access the stack frame using the `sp` register without incurring the problem of changing offsets and without the overhead of maintaining the `fp` register. In addition, with this approach, we now use only one `addi` instruction to allocate stack space rather than a separate `addi` instruction to allocate space for each push or reserve operation.

Calling a Subroutine

A program typically consists of several routines, with some routines calling others. We refer to a routine that calls another as a *caller*. We refer to a routine that is called as a *callee* or *subroutine*. If a callee in turn calls a routine, then it is both a callee and a caller. For example, the program in `r0308.a` consists of three routines labeled with `_start`, `sub1`, and `sub2`. The `_start` routine calls `sub1` which in turn calls `sub2`. Thus, `_start` is a caller, `sub1` is both a callee and a caller, and `sub2` is a callee.

To call a subroutine given the label on its starting instruction, we use the `jal` instruction. For example, the `jal` instruction on line 1 in `r0308.a` calls `sub1`. The `jal` instruction also saves the return address (i.e., the address `sub1` should return to) in the `ra` register. The return address is the address of the instruction that follows the `jal` instruction. Thus, for the `jal` instruction on line 1, the return address is the address of the `halt` instruction.

Because the `jal` instruction on line 7 overlays the return address in `ra` with a new return address (with the address `sub2` needs to return to `sub1`), `sub1` has to save the return address it needs and then restore it into `ra` before it executes the `jalr` instruction on line 14. It does this on entry by pushing the return address in `ra` onto the stack (lines 4 and 5), and popping it back into `ra` (lines 12 and 13) just before the jalr instruction on line 14 is executed. sub2 does not execute any instructions that modify the return address in ra. Thus, unlike sub1, it does not have to save and restore the return address in ra.

Rule: On entry, a caller should push the return address in ra onto the stack, and then pop it back into the ra just before its returning jalr instruction is executed. A callee that is not also a caller should *not* do this.

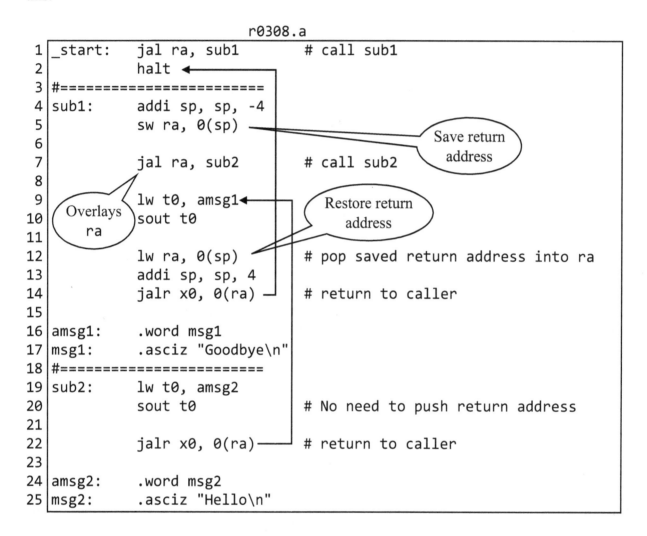

r0308.a

```
 1 _start:    jal ra, sub1      # call sub1
 2            halt
 3 #========================
 4 sub1:      addi sp, sp, -4
 5            sw ra, 0(sp)
 6
 7            jal ra, sub2      # call sub2
 8
 9            lw t0, amsg1
10            sout t0
11
12            lw ra, 0(sp)      # pop saved return address into ra
13            addi sp, sp, 4
14            jalr x0, 0(ra)    # return to caller
15
16 amsg1:     .word msg1
17 msg1:      .asciz "Goodbye\n"
18 #========================
19 sub2:      lw t0, amsg2
20            sout t0           # No need to push return address
21
22            jalr x0, 0(ra)    # return to caller
23
24 amsg2:     .word msg2
25 msg2:      .asciz "Hello\n"
```

Callouts in figure: "Save return address", "Overlays ra", "Restore return address"

The program in r0308.a displays

Hello
Goodbye

What is displayed if line 7 is moved to line 11? Modify and run the program to check your answer. What happens if line 12 in the original program is commented out? Modify and run the program to check your answer.

Shift Instructions

Consider the following `addi` instruction:

```
addi t0, t0, 5
```

The `rv` assembler translates this instruction by first converting its components—the mnemonic and the three operands—to the binary sequences they represent and then inserting the resulting binary sequences into the machine language instruction. For example, the assembler converts the third operand to the binary equivalent of 5 decimal, which is 0...0101. However, before the assembler can insert this binary number into the machine instruction, it has to position it to the where it belongs in the machine instruction. It goes into the immediate field whose rightmost bit is in position 20 in the instruction. Because the rightmost bit of the binary equivalent of 5 decimal is in position 0, it has to be shifted left 20 positions to the left (so it is in position 20) before it can be inserted into the machine instruction.

Although shift operations are not needed by most programs, for some programs, as the example in the preceding paragraph illustrates, shift operations are essential. In RISC-V, the shift instructions come in pairs:

`slli`	shift left logical immediate	
`sll`	shift left logical	logical shift instructions (inject 0)
`srli`	shift right logical immediate	
`srl`	shift right logical	
`srai`	shift right arithmetic immediate	arithmetic shift instructions (inject sign bit)
`sra`	shift right arithmetic	

The immediate-type of shift instructions (`slli`, `srli`, `srai`) specify the *shift amount*—the number of positions to shift—with an immediate value. The non-immediate-type of shift instructions (`sll`, `srl`, `sra`) specify a register that holds the shift amount. For example, the instruction,

```
slli t0, t1, 15 # shift amount is 15
```

shifts left a copy of the contents of the second register (`t1`). The shift amount is the immediate value (15). The result of the shift is loaded into the first register (`t0`). The `sll` (shift left logical) instruction is similar, except its third operand specifies a register that holds the shift amount:

```
sll t0, t1, t2   # shift amount is in t2
```

The logical shift instructions (`sll`, `slli`, `srl`, `srli`) shift 0's into the positions vacated by the shift operation. For example, if 110...101 is logically shifted right one position, the result is 0110...10. If a negative number is logically right shifted, its sign bit becomes 0. Thus, the shifted number becomes positive. The arithmetic shift instructions (`sra`, `srai`), on the other hand, fill the positions vacated by the shift operation with a copy of the sign bit of the number before the shift. Thus, if the sign bit is 1, it remains 1. For example, if 110...101 is arithmetically shifted right one position, the result is 1110...10. Its sign bit remains 1. Thus, the number remains negative.

All the shift instructions use the R-type format. The immediate type of shift instruction uses the *rs2* field to hold the shift amount. The non-immediate type use the *rs2* field to specify the register that holds the shift amount:

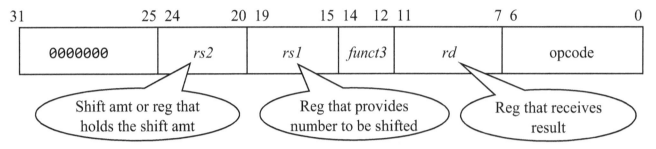

For example, the machine instruction for the `slli` instruction

```
slli t0, t1, 15 # shift amount is 15
```

is

```
 funct7    rs2    rs1 funct3  rd    opcode
0000000  01111  00110  001  00101  0010011
```

The *rs2* field is treated as an unsigned number. Thus, the shift amount that the *rs2* field can specify range from 0 to 31. In both types, the *rs1* field specifies the register that provides the number to be shifted, and the *rd* field specifies the register to receive the result.

Left shifting a number in a register with `sll` or `slli` has the same effect as multiplying it by 2. For example, if we shift 0…011 (3 decimal) left one position, we get 0…0110 (6 decimal). Thus, left shifting *n* positions has the effect of multiplying the number by 2^n (as long as the result can fit into the destination register). Right shifting a number in a register with logical right shift instruction—either `srl` or `srli`— has the effect of dividing a non-negative number by 2. However, right shifting a negative number with a logical right shift instruction does *not* divide the number by 2. It injects 0's from the left, making the resulting number positive. The arithmetic right shift instructions maintain the sign bit so they do not make the number go positive. But unfortunately, they do not give the correct answer if the number divided is a negative odd number. For example, if 11…1001 (−7 decimal) is arithmetically shifted right one position, the result is 11…1100, which equals −4. But −7 divided by 2 should equal −3. However, the division by 2 performed by the right arithmetic shift instructions is consistent with an alternate definition of division (favored by some algebraists) that requires the remainder be non-negative. With this alternate definition, -7/2 = -4 with a remainder = +1. But this definition is not the operative definition of division in the computer world.

In addition to dividing by 2, the arithmetic shift instructions are used to sign extend a value. For example, suppose `t0` holds a 12-bit immediate value that needs to be sign extended. To do that, we simply shift `t0` left 20 positions to put its sign bit in the leftmost position of `t0`. Then arithmetic shift right 20 positions:

```
slli t0, t0, 20  # position sign bit in leftmost bit of t0
srai t0, t0, 20  # shift back to orig position which extending
```

The right shift not only puts the immediate value back to its original position but also extends its sign by replicating its sign bit.

The shift instructions can also be used to multiply a number. For example, to multiply a number by 3, we can shift it one position to the left (to multiply it by 2). Then add the original number to the shifted number to get 3 times the original number. Using this technique, the program r0309.a multiplies the number entered from the keyboard by 3 and displays the result. This program reads in number into a0 and then calls the mult3 subroutine, passing it the number to multiply in a0. We call the values we pass to a subroutine *arguments*. Thus, this program passes one argument (the number to multiply) to the subroutine via the a0 register. The subroutine uses a slli and an add instruction to multiply the number in a0 by 3. It then returns to the caller with the product in a0. Thus, in this program the caller uses a0 to pass the argument to the subroutine. The subroutine also uses a0 to pass the *return value* (i.e., the computed result) back to the caller.

```
                                  r0309.a
 1          lw t0, aprompt  # load address of prompt message
 2          sout t0         # display prompt message
 3          din a0          # input number to multiply
 4          jal ra, multby3 # call subroutne
 5          lw t0, amsg     # get address of label
 6          sout t0         # label answer
 7          dout a0         # display answer
 8          halt
 9 prompt:   .asciz "Enter decimal number\n"
10 aprompt: .word prompt
11 msg:      .asciz "product = "
12 amsg:     .word msg
13 #=======================================================
14 multby3:  addi t0, a0, 0  # move a0 to t0
15           slli a0, a0, 1  # multiply number by 2
16           add a0, a0, t0  # add the original number to get 3 times
17           jalr x0, 0(ra)  # return to the caller with answer in a0
```

When the jal instruction on line 4 is executed, it loads the specified register (ra in this example) with the return address (the address of line 5). The operand "0(ra)" in the jalr instruction on line 17 indicates that the jump-to address is given by the address in ra plus the offset 0. Thus, the jalr jumps to the return address in the ra register—to line 5. A jalr instruction, like the jal instruction, normally loads a return address in the register specified by its first operand. But on line 17, we do not want the jalr instruction to do that. So we specify x0 as the first operand. Recall that the contents of x0 is permanently set to 0. Thus, the jalr instruction does not load any register with a new return address. It simply returns to the return address in ra.

You may be wondering why the registers have aliases? Why not simply use their "x" names exclusively? Except for x0, sp, gp, and tp, they are all general purpose. So one register is just as good as another for any given application. We use aliases for registers to reflect their typical use. For example, the "a" registers (i.e., the registers whose aliases start with the letter "a") by convention are used to pass arguments to a subroutine ("a" is for "argument). The ra register by convention is used to hold the return address in a subroutine call ("ra" is for "return address"). The "t" registers are used to temporarily hold values ("t" is for "temporary"). For example, t0 in r0309.a is used by the caller to hold the address for the sout instruction (see line 1). Once the sout instruction is executed, the value in t0 is no longer needed. The caller again uses t0 to hold the address for the second sout instruction (see line 5). Here again, t0 is used to hold a value only temporarily. Note that the subroutine also uses t0 (see lines 14 and 16). Thus, a caller should not assume that what it puts in a "t" register is still there after a subroutine call. We also want some registers that are guaranteed not to be corrupted by a subroutine call. Thus, for these registers, the subroutine should either not modify them, or, if it does, first save their contents, then modify them, then restore them with their original contents before returning to the caller. By convention, the "s" registers used in this way ("s" is for "saved").

Test the program in r0309.a with both positive and negative values. Does it work for negative values as well as positive values?

Set-Compare Instructions

The branch instructions perform a compare operation and then a conditional branch based on the result. The branch instructions have two limitations. First, they perform only register-to-register comparisons—they do not perform register-to-immediate value comparisons. Thus, if we want to compare the contents of t0 with 5, we first have to load 5 into some register. Second, the branch instructions all include a conditional branch. Generally, after a comparison, we want a conditional branch. But sometimes we want to perform several comparisons before the conditional branch (we give an example of this in the section on overflow that follows). We cannot do that with a branch instruction.

To provide more flexibility in performing branches, RISC-V has the set-compare instructions: slti (set if less than immediate), sltiu (set if less than immediate unsigned), slt (set if less than), and sltu (set if less than unsigned). All four of these instructions set the destination register to 1 if the result of the comparison is true, and to 0 otherwise. For example, consider the following instruction:

```
slti t0, t1, 5   # compare t1 and 5, result (1 or 0) into t0
```

If the contents of t1 is less than 5, then t0 is set to 1. Otherwise it is set 0.

The slti and sltiu instructions use the I-type format (*imm[11:0], rs1, funct3, rd, opcode*). The slt and sltu instructions use the R-type format (*funct7, rs2, rs1, funct3, rd, opcode*).

Recall that signed and unsigned comparisons can give different results with the same numbers. For example all 1's represents −1 as a signed number. but it represents a large positive number as an unsigned number. Thus, all 1's is less than 0 in a signed comparison, but greater than 0 in an unsigned comparison. slt and slti perform signed comparisons. That is, slt treats the numbers in the *rs1* and *rs2* registers as signed numbers. slti treats the number is *rs1* and the immediate value as signed numbers. sltu and sltiu perform unsigned comparisons. That is, sltu treats the numbers in the *rs1* and *rs2* registers as unsigned numbers. sltiu treats the number in the *rs1* register and the immediate value *after it has been signed extended* as unsigned numbers.

Although all the set-comparisons perform a "less than" comparison, you can use them to determine if a register is equal to 0 or equal to 1. Consider the following instruction:

```
sltiu t0, t1, 1  # t0 set to 1 if contents of t1 are zero
```

Because this instruction performs an unsigned comparison, the only way the contents of t1 can be less than 1 if it is 0. Thus, it sets t0 to 1 if the contents of t1 is zero. Otherwise, it sets t0 to 0. To determine if the contents of t1 is nonzero, use

```
sltu t0, x0, t1  # t0 set to 1 if contents of t1 are nonzero.
```

If the contents of `t1` are nonzero, then the contents of `x0` (which is 0) are less than the contents of `t1` when treated as an unsigned number. Thus, this instruction sets `t0` to 1 if the contents of `t1` are nonzero. Otherwise it sets `t0` to 0.

Detecting Overflow

Recall from Chapter 1 that overflow can occur if

- two unsigned numbers are added and the result is too big to fit into the destination register
- two unsigned number are subtracted and the result is negative (so the number cannot be represented as an unsigned number).
- two signed numbers are added or subtracted and the result is either too positive or too negative to fit into the destination register.

Most programs do not test for the possibility of overflow because they process numbers that will never cause overflow. For example, consider a program that computes the average test grade in a class that never has more than 100 students. To compute the average, it has to sum at most 100 grades between 0 and 100, then divide by the number of grades. Obviously, the sum of 100 grades cannot exceed the capacity of a 32-bit register, which is approximately 4 billion for an unsigned number. However, if in a computation, we do need to test for overflow, we can do so with the appropriate instructions in the RISC-V instruction. Let consider several cases:

Case 1: Adding two unsigned numbers in `t1` and `t2`. `t0` receives the result.
Overflow has occurred if and only if a carry out of the leftmost position (bit 31 in a 32-bit register) has occurred. This bit represents the value 2^{32}. Because the carry bit is lost if overflow occurs, the sum is too small by 2^{32}. The `t2` number that is added to the `t1` number can be no greater than $2^{32}-1$ (the largest 32-bit unsigned number). Thus, the sum in `t0` is

$$\text{t1 number } + \text{ (at most } 2^{31}-1) - \text{ (the lost value } 2^{32})$$

which is necessarily less than the number in `t1`. If, on the other hand, overflow does not occur, then the sum must be greater than or equal to the number in `t1` (because the non-negative number in `t2` is added to `t1`). Thus, overflow has occurred if and only if the sum in `t0` is less than the number in `t1`. We can test for this result with a `bltu` instruction:

```
add t0, t1, t2
bltu t0, t1, overflow  # branch if sum in t0 less than t1 number
```

Case 2: Subtracting the unsigned number in `t2` from the unsigned number in `t1`. `t0` receives result.
Overflow occurs if and only if the `t1` number is less than the `t2` number (so the result is negative and therefore cannot be represented by an unsigned number). We can test for this condition in advance (i.e., before the subtraction) using a `bltu` instruction:

```
bltu t1, t2, overflow  # branch if t1 number less than t2 number
sub t0, t1, t2
```

Case 3: Adding a signed number in `t2` to the signed number in `t1`. `t0` receives the result.

If the t2 number is negative, the sum should be less than the t1 number (because the sum is t1 plus a negative number). If not, overflow has occurred. If the t2 number is *not* negative, then the sum should *not* be less than the t1 number (because the sum is t1 plus a non-negative number). If not, overflow has occurred. In other words (using the register names to represent their contents), overflow has occurred if and only if

      t2 < 0 is true and t0 < t1 is false.

or

      t2 < 0 is false and t0 < t1 is true.

or even more succinctly, overflow has occurred if and only if

      (t2 < 0) not equal to (t0 < t1)

We can evaluate the last expression using two set-comparison instructions for the "<" comparisons, and a bne instruction for the "not equal" comparison:

```
    add t0, t1, t2
    slti t3, t2, 0        # t3 = (t2 < 0)
    slt t4, t0, t1        # t4 = (t0 < t1)
    bne t3, t4, overflow  # branch t3 not equal to t4
```

A minor modification to this code gives the test for signed overflow in a subtraction. Incidentally, the code above is an example of the utility of the set-compare instructions. To test for overflow, we do not need a conditional branch after the first two comparisons. The set-compare instructions provide the RISC-V with that capability.

Byte and Halfword Load and Store Instructions

The byte and halfword load and store instructions work like and have the same format as the lw and sw instructions, but operate on byte and halfword operands instead of word operands. lb (load byte) loads a single byte, sign extended to 32 bits, into the specified register. lbu (load byte unsigned) also loads a single byte but zero extends it to 32 bits. Similarly, lh (load half) and lhu (load half unsigned) load half words, sign extended by lh or zero extended by lhu. sb (store byte) and sh (store half) store the rightmost byte or halfword, respectively, in the specified register. Like lw and sw, all these byte and halfword load and store instructions can dereference pointers.

In the following program, the lb instruction is used to access the successive characters of the inputted string. The program counts and displays the number of occurrences of the capital letter "A".

r0310.a

```
 1           lw t0, aprompt     # get address of prompt
 2           sout t0            # prompt user
 3           lw t0, abuffer     # get address of buffer
 4           sin t0             # read in string
 5           addi t2, x0, 0     # set count to 0
 6 loop:     lb t1, 0(t0)       # get char from string
 7           beq t1, x0, done   # branch if null char
 8           addi t1, t1, -'A'  # subtract letter A
 9           sltiu t1, t1, 1    # test if result is 0
10           add t2, t2, t1     # add 1 or 0 to count
11           addi t0, t0, 1     # move str pointer to next char
12           jal x0, loop       # unconditional jump
13 done:     lw t0, amsg        # get address of msg
14           sout t0            # display msg
15           dout t2            # display count
16           halt
17 aprompt:  .word prompt
18 prompt:   .asciz "Enter string\n"
19 amsg:     .word msg
20 msg:      .asciz "Count = "
21 abuffer:  .word buffer
22 buffer:   .zero 100
```

After inputting a string (line 4) and setting the count in t2 to 0 (line 5), the program executes a loop. When the loop starts, t0 has the address of the first character in the string, and t2 (the count) is 0. The first instruction in the loop (line 6) loads t1 with the character t0 points to. Each time through the loop, line 11 adds 1 to t0. Thus, each time line 6 is executed, it loads the next character in the inputted string. Line 7 tests if the character loaded is the null character, which indicates the end of the string. If the character is the null character, the beq instruction branches out of the loop. If not, the addi instruction on line 8 subtracts the ASCII code for "A" (by adding its negation) from the ASCII code of the character just loaded into t0 by line 6. If the result is 0, then the character just loaded by line 6 must be the capital letter "A". The sltiu instruction of line 9 tests if the result is 0 (note that if the number in t1, treated as an unsigned number, is less than 1, it must be 0). If the result of the subtraction is 0, the sltiu instruction sets t1 to 1, which is then used on line 10 to increment the count in t2. If, on the other hand, the result of the subtraction is not 0 (which means the character from the inputted string is not the capital letter "A"), the sltiu instruction sets t1 to 0. The add instruction on line 10 then has no effect on the count in t2. Line 11 then increments t0 so it points to the next character in the string. Line 12 unconditionally jumps back to the beginning of the loop. Line 15 displays the final count.

Big Endian Versus Little Endian

Each slot in memory holds one byte (i.e., 8 bits). Thus, storing a 32-bit word in memory requires four memory slots. There are two ways that are commonly used to store a 32-bit word in memory. Because the weights of the bits in a number increase from right to left, the right side of a number is called the *little end*, and the left side the *big end*. One way is to store the word in consecutive memory locations starting with the little-end byte (i.e, the rightmost byte of the number). For example, if 12345678 hex is stored in the word in memory at the address 100, it would look like this:

```
~   ~
| 78 | 100        Little endian (little end first)
| 56 | 101
| 34 | 102
| 13 | 103
~   ~
```

We call this approach the *little-endian* approach. A computer that uses it is called a called a *little-endian computer*.

The other commonly used approach is to store a word starting with the big-end byte (i.e., the leftmost byte). If 12345678 hex is stored in the word in memory at the address 100, it would look like this:

```
~   ~
| 12 | 100        Big Endian (big end first)
| 34 | 101
| 56 | 102
| 78 | 103
~   ~
```

We call this approach the *big-endian* approach. A computer that uses it is called a called a *big-endian computer*. RISC-V is little-endian.

The little-endian approach has some advantages. One advantage is that it simplifies the conversion of a word integer to a halfword integer. For example, suppose the type `int` and `short` map to 32- and 16-bit quantities, respectively. Now consider what happens when we execute the following sequence on a little-endian computer:

```
short y;
int x = 0x00001234;
y = (short)x;        // assign lower word in x to y
```

The halfword at the address of x is the lower halfword in the variable x. This the halfword to be assigned to y. However, on a big-endian computer, the halfword at the address x is the higher halfword—*not* the halfword to be assigned to y. The halfword we want (the lower halfword) is at the address of x *plus* 2 on a big-endian computer. Thus, the assignment of x to y requires an address computation at some point (the address of x and 2 have to be added) on a big-endian computer, but not on a little-endian computer.

Another advantage of the little-endian approach comes into play when we want to process the bytes that make up a word in rightmost-to-leftmost order. For example, we do this when we perform multi-byte addition byte by byte. On a little-endian computer, the address of the word is also the address of the rightmost byte. But on a big-endian computer, the address of the word is the address of the leftmost byte. Thus, on a big-endian computer, we have to perform an address computation to get the address of the starting byte.

Neither of the "advantages" of a little-endian computer cited above amount to much. Perhaps, the most important advantage (and only advantage of any significance) of the little-endian approach is compatibility with most of the computers that are in use today. IBM mainframes are big endian, but most everything else is little endian (a few are bi-endian).

One of the annoying aspects of a little-endian computer not shared by a big-endian computer is that memory dumps show the bytes that make up a word in right-to-left order (because that is the order in which they are stored in memory on a little-endian computer). Thus, the bytes appear in a dump in reverse order. For example, a hex memory dump of the machine code for the following program

```
        halt
        .word 0x12345678
```
is

```
  00 00 00 00 78 56 34 12
  ‾‾‾‾‾‾‾‾‾‾‾
  halt instruction
```

Note that the bytes for the constant 12345678 hex appear in reverse order.

One advantage of a big-endian computer is that it can more easily use its numeric compare instructions to compare strings. For example, suppose two four-character strings are loaded into registers t0 and t1. On a big-endian computer, the characters in the registers will be in the same order as they are in memory (because the first character in the string goes into the high-order byte of the register). But on a little-endian computer, the strings will be in reverse order (because the first character in the string goes into the low-order byte of the register). For example, the string "ABCD" will be loaded into t0 as "ABCD" on a big-endian computer and as "DCBA" on a little-endian computer.

On a big-endian computer, if the contents of the registers that hold strings are treated as unsigned numbers, the number in t0 will be less than the number in t1 if and only if the string in t0 alphabetically precedes the string in t1. Thus, we can use the numeric comparison instructions to determine alphabetical order. However, this is not the case on a little-endian computer. For example, suppose "ABCD" and "EFGH" are loaded into t0 and t1, respectively. If the contents of t0 and t1 are treated as 32-bit unsigned numbers and compared, on both a big-endian and little-endian computer, t0 will be less that t1, which correctly indicates that the t0 string alphabetically precedes the t1 string. But now suppose "AAAD" and "BBBA" are loaded into t0 and t1, respectively, and compared. On a big-endian computer, t0 will be less than t1, correctly indicating that the t0 string alphabetically precedes the t1 string. But on a little-endian computer, t0 will be greater than t1 because t0 contains "DAAA" and t1 contains "ABBB", *incorrectly* indicating that the t0 string alphabetically follows the t1 string. The simple solution to this problem is to compare strings byte by byte on a little-endian computer rather than word by word. Moreover, the code that compares strings word by word is complicated—because the length of a string is not necessarily a multiple of the length of a word. For this reason, string compares are almost always done byte by byte, even on a big-endian computer. Thus, in the final analysis, big endian intrinsically is no better that little endian, and vice versa. The only important consideration is compatibility with other types of computers. Because little endian is the dominant byte ordering scheme among modern computers, it was chosen for the RISC-V.

Debugger Commands

The debugger provided by the rv program is a full-featured debugger. If the input file is an assembly language program (i.e., an ".a" file as opposed to an ".e." executable file), the debugger acts as a *symbolic debugger*. That is, it allows the use of labels from the source program in lieu of their addresses, and shows the source program form of instructions as they are executed. For example, to show the memory location corresponding to the label xyz, simply enter at the debugger's prompt,

```
        mxyz
```

You can also use the actual address of xyz in place of the label xyz in the m command, but it is much simpler to use the label instead.

Numbers entered in debugger commands *are assumed to be in hex*, except for the register number in a "x" register name and the debugger command that changes the step count. For example, the "12" in "x12" is a decimal number. However, the base of a number entered can be explicitly specified by prefixing a decimal number with #, and hex number with 0x, and a binary number with 0b. For example,

```
m #3000 0b1010
```

displays 1010 (binary) words starting at the address 3000 (decimal).

If the -d command line argument is specified when rv is invoked, the rv program pauses when the interpretation of the assembled program is about to start. In addition, the trace function is turned on, the step count is set to 1, and the debugger is activated. Thus, each time the Enter key is hit, rv executes and traces one instruction. At any pause, any of the following commands can be entered (note that labels can be used in these commands as indicated only if the input file is an assembly language file):

Hit Enter key
> Run, pausing each time step-count number of instructions is executed and at breakpoints.

n (where *n* is an integer)
> Set step count to *n*, and then execute *n* instructions. For example, if 5 is entered, then the debugger executes five instructions and then pauses. Each time the Enter key is subsequently hit, the debugger executes five instructions and then pauses.

b <address or label>
> Sets a breakpoint at the specified address or label, replacing the current breakpoint, if any. When execution reaches a breakpoint, the debugger is activated and execution is paused.

b Display current breakpoint.

b- Cancel the current breakpoint.

c <reg, address, or label> <new value>
> Change a value in a register or a memory location.

g Set step count to infinity and run, pausing only at breakpoints and watchpoints, if any.

h Help screen

i Display instruction to be executed next.

i<address or label> Display instruction at address or label.

m Display all memory in use.

m <address or label> <count> Display count lines of memory.

q Quit program.

x   Display all registers.

x<reg name or number> Display specified register.

s   Display stack.

t   Turn instruction trace on (trace is off on startup unless -t or -d is specified on the command line).

t- turn instruction trace off.

w<address or label>
> Set watchpoint at specified label or address. When a store into the location specified by a watchpoint occurs, the debugger is activated and execution is paused.

w   Display current watchpoint.

w- cancel the current watchpoint.

z   Set step count to infinity and run to the end of the program, ignoring breakpoints and watchpoints.

Setting a breakpoint with the b debugger command is particularly helpful for debugging. For example, suppose the assembler displays an error message on the instruction at location 100. To find out more about the error, run the program again with the debugger on (specify the -d command line argument when you invoke rv). On activation of the debugger, immediately enter

```
b 100
```

to set a breakpoint at the location of the problem. Then enter

```
g
```

to execute at full speed. When the breakpoint is reached, execution is paused, at which point you can use the debugger to examine register and memory contents to determine the source of the problem.

When the debugger is active, everything that is displayed on the screen is also written to the ".lst" and ".bst" files. A convenient way to debug offline, is to run the program with the trace active (specify the -t command line argument when invoking rv). Then print out the ".lst" file, which will contain the trace for the entire run. Then using the listing, you can debug your program at your leisure at your favorite location.

For complete information on the debugger, see the file rv.txt.

Problems

Note: Be sure that your programs prompt for any user input and label any output.

1) The program in r0305.a goes acts erratically for some inputs. Fix this problem by changing just one instruction.

2) Write and run an assembly language program that reads in a positive number and displays your name that number of times. Test your program by entering 10.

3) Write and run an assembly language program that repeatedly prompts for and reads in decimal numbers until a negative number is entered, at which point your program should display the sum of all the numbers previously entered. Test your program by entering 1, 2, 3, −1 (the sum displayed should be 6).

4) Write and run an assembly language program that prompts for and reads in a positive decimal number and then displays the sum of all the integers from 1 to the number entered. Test your program by entering 10.

5) Write and run an assembly language program that displays a table of ASCII codes from 32 to 126 and their corresponding characters. *Hint*: Use dout and aout inside a loop.

6) Write and run an assembly language program that reads in 10 decimal numbers and displays the largest. Test your program by entering 3, 100, −30, −50, 101, 99, 0, −1, 5, 77.

7) Write and run an assembly language program that prompts for and reads in a string. It should then call subroutine 1, passing it the address of the string in a0. Subroutine 1 should display the string whose address it is passed with all uppercase letters changed to lowercase, and then call subroutine 2, passing it the address of the modified string in a0. Subroutine 2 should then display the string whose address it is passed with all letters in uppercase. Test your program with "Aa1Bb2Cc3{+".

8) Write and run an assembly language program that prompts for and reads in a string, and passes its address to a subroutine via a0. Your subroutine should then display all and only the decimal digits in the string. Test your program with "Aa1Bb2Cc3{+".

9) Write and run an assembly language program that reads in a hex number and passes its address to a subroutine via a0. Your subroutine should display the number in binary. Test your program by entering 3210BCD. Display the binary number with a space between each group of four bits.

10) Write and run an assembly language program that reads in a four-bit binary number (with spaces separating the bits) and displays its equivalent hex digit. Test your program by entering 0 1 0 1.

11) Write and run an assembly language program which reads in a number and displays the number of 1-bits in its 32-bit binary representation. Test your program with 0, 1, −1, 255, and −5000.

12) Write and run an assembly language program that reads in two integers, calls using a jal instruction a subroutine passing the two numbers in a0 an a1. Your subroutine should add the two numbers and return the sum via a0 to its caller. The caller then should display the sum. It should then call a second

subroutine passing it the same two numbers, but this time using the `jalr` instruction to call the subroutine. Your second subroutine should determine and return the larger number to its caller. The caller should then display the larger number. Test your program with the pair 2, 3.

13) The only actual restriction on the placement of an `.equ` directive is that it must precede any `li` instruction or any `.zero` or `.space` directive that uses the equated name. Why does this restriction apply only to the `li` instruction and the `.zero` and `.space` directives? How can the assembler be modified so that there are no restrictions at all on the placement of `.equ` directives?

14) Write and run an assembly language program that reads in a hex number. It should left shift the inputted number so its leftmost 1-bit is in position 31 in a register. It should then arithmetic right shift the number so it back in its original position. Display the resulting number in hex. Test your program with 0 (result should be 0), 1, −1, 16, 32, and 128.

15) Write and run an assembly language program that reads in a number, multiplies it by 7 using a sequence of shift and add instructions, and displays the result. Test your program with 5, −5, and 0.

16) Write and run an assembly language program that reads in two signed integers, adds them, and displays OVERFLOW (if overflow occurs) or NO OVERFLOW (if no overflow occurs). Test your program with the following pairs: (0x1, 0x7fffffff), (0xffffffff, 0x80000000), (0x5, 0xfffffff0), (0x15, 0xffffffff), (0x5, 0x15), (0xfffffff0, 0xffffffff).

17) Same as problem 16 but subtract.

18) Same as problem 16 but treat the numbers as unsigned numbers.

19) Same as problem 16 but treat the numbers as unsigned numbers and subtract.

20) Is the following instruction legal:

```
add t0, t1, 1
```

Try assembling it using `rv`. What happens?

4 Assembly Language Part 2

Register Use Conventions

Suppose a program consists of a routine (the "caller") which calls a subroutine (the "callee"). The caller will likely keep its variables in registers so that it executes more quickly than if its variables were in memory. For the same reason, the callee will also want to keep its variables in registers. But how can the callee use the same registers that the caller uses without destroying the caller's values in those registers? One approach that works well is to designate a subset of the available registers as callee-saved registers, and a second subset, disjoint from the first, as caller-saved registers. A *callee-saved register* is a register that the callee saves and restores, but only if it modifies it. Thus, a callee-saved register is *preserved across a call*. That is, its after-call value is guaranteed to be the same as its before-call value. A *caller-saved register* is a register for which the callee has no obligation to preserve across the call. Thus, if the caller needs it preserved across the call, it is the caller that has to preserve it (by saving it before the call and restoring it after the call).

The terminology "callee-saved" and "caller-saved" can be somewhat misleading. The callee does not necessarily save a callee-saved register. The callee saves (and restores) a callee-saved register only if it modifies the register. Similarly, the caller does not necessarily save a caller-saved register. The caller saves (and restores) a caller-saved register only if the caller needs it preserved across a call.

It is advantageous to have both callee-saved registers and caller-saved registers. Here are two scenarios. In the first, a caller-saved register is better; in the second a callee-saved register is better.

- Suppose that the caller is using a register that it does not have to be preserved across a call. If the register is a caller-saved register, then it will not be unnecessarily saved and restored. Neither the caller nor the callee will save and restore it. But if the register is callee-saved, the callee will unnecessarily save it if it modifies it. Thus, in this scenario, a caller-saved register is better.

- Suppose the caller is using a register that has to be preserved across a call. If the register is a callee-saved register, it will be saved and restored by the callee, but *only if* necessary (i.e., only if the callee modifies it). But if the register is caller-saved, the caller would have to save and restore it, even if it is not necessary, because the callee might modify the register. Thus, in this scenario, a callee-saved register is better.

In RISC-V, by convention, the callee-saved registers are sp and s0 through s11 (note that their aliases all start with the letter "s"). The caller-saved registers are ra, t0 through t6, and a0 through a7. The registers which are neither are x0, gp, and tp (these registers have special purposes and should not be used as general-purpose registers).

The registers a0 through a7 are used by the caller to pass up to eight arguments to the caller. If there are more than eight arguments, the arguments after the eighth are passed via the stack. That is, the caller pushes them on the stack, and the callee accesses them from the stack. Accessing arguments on the stack is much slower than accessing them in registers. But because calls rarely pass more than eight arguments, using the stack to pass arguments is usually unnecessary. The registers a0 through a7 are caller-saved. Thus, if the caller wants their values preserved across a subroutine call, it must save them before the call and restore them afterwards. a0 and a1 are also used to return up to two values back to the caller.

The ra register is a caller-saved register. A caller must save and restore the ra register because the call it makes overlays the return address in ra that it needs to return to its caller. A callee that is not also a caller, on the other hand, does not modify the `ra` register. Thus, it should not save and restore the `ra` register.

The "`t`" registers are caller-saved. They are typically used to hold a value temporarily and therefore rarely need to be preserved across a call. For example, consider the code to display the string at the label `msg`:

```
        lw t0, amsg        # load t0 with address of msg
        sout t0            # value in t0 not needed after this instruction
            ⋮
msg:    .asciz "Hi"
amsg:   .word msg
```

After the `sout` instruction is executed, the address in `t0` is no longer needed. Thus, if a call subsequently occurs, `t0` does not need to be saved and restored by the caller.

Header in an Executable File

The program in `r0401.a` consists of a caller that starts on line 7 and the called subroutine that starts on line 1. When this program is executed, we expect the following behavior:

1. the caller calls the subroutine
2. the subroutine displays "Hi"
3. the subroutine returns to the caller.
4. the caller halts.

Thus, its intended effect is to display a single occurrence of "Hi". However, the program has a bug—an infinite loop. If it is loaded into memory starting at the address 0, instead of displaying a single "Hi" and halting, it displays "Hi" repeatedly.

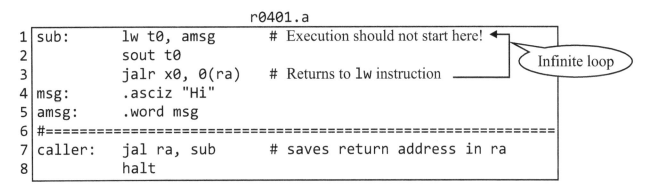

r0401.a

```
1 sub:       lw t0, amsg        # Execution should not start here!
2            sout t0
3            jalr x0, 0(ra)     # Returns to lw instruction
4 msg:       .asciz "Hi"
5 amsg:      .word msg
6 #==============================================================
7 caller:    jal ra, sub        # saves return address in ra
8            halt
```

When the `rv` program (acting as the operating system) loads the program in `r0401.a` into memory, it starts its execution at the load point. Thus, the instruction at the physical beginning of the program is the first instruction to be executed. If the program in `r0401.a` is loaded into memory starting at address 0, its execution incorrectly starts at address 0—*with the subroutine*, not the caller code. It displays "Hi" and then executes the `jalr` instruction on line 3. Because the subroutine was never called by the `jal` instruction on line 7, `ra` does not have a valid return address. It contains its initial value 0. Thus, when executed, the `jalr` instruction jumps to address 0, and the subroutine is again executed. When the `jalr` instruction is again executed, it again jumps to address 0 and again the subroutine is executed. This sequence is repeated without stopping until the `rv` program suspects an infinite loop and forces a pause in execution.

What is the fix for the infinite loop in the program above? We, of course, can reorder the subroutine and the caller so that the caller is first. But what if we want to keep the subroutine first? No problem. Simply change the label at the start of the caller code to `_start`:

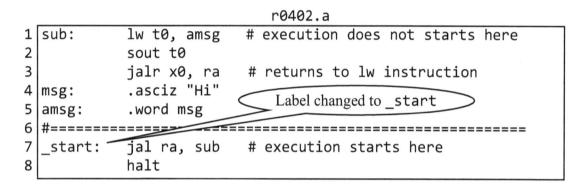

r0402.a

```
1 sub:        lw t0, amsg    # execution does not starts here
2             sout t0
3             jalr x0, ra    # returns to lw instruction
4 msg:        .asciz "Hi"
5 amsg:       .word msg              Label changed to _start
6 #=========================================================
7 _start:     jal ra, sub    # execution starts here
8             halt
```

The *entry point* of a program is the point within a program at which execution starts. The label `_start` is a special label that marks the entry point of a program. Thus, with the label `_start` on line 7, execution starts with the `jal` instruction on that line, which calls the subroutine. Then after displaying one "Hi", the subroutine executes the `jalr` instruction, which now returns to the `halt` instruction on line 8, terminating execution. No more infinite loop.

The `_start` label does *not* affect the machine code to which the program is translated by the assembler. This observation leads us to the following interesting question: How does the `rv` program acting as the operating system know where the entry point is when it loads into memory the executable form of the program? We can find the answer to this question in `r0402.lst`(the ".lst" file for this program). The machine code for the program is not affected by the `_start` label. However, the header in the file that contains the executable program is affected: It now has an `S` entry ("S" is for "start") which specifies the entry point relative to the beginning of the machine code for the program. An `S` entry consists of the letter `S` following by the entry point address. After the `rv` program loads in a program with an `S` entry in the header, it starts execution of the program at the location given by the load point plus the entry point address in the `S` entry. For example, if the `rv` program loads the executable form of the program in `r0402.a` into memory starting at the address 300 hex, then it starts execution at 300 + address in the `S` entry = 300 + 0014 = 314, which is the start of the caller routine.

r0402.lst

```
rv Version 3.4                        Tue Aug  6 07:46:14 2019
Anthony J. Dos Reis


Header
R
A 00000010
S 00000014
C


Loc     Code           Source Code
0000    0101a283 sub:       lw t0, amsg    # execution does not starts here
0004    0c028000            sout t0
0008    00008067            jalr x0, ra    # returns to lw instruction
000c    00006948 msg:       .asciz "Hi"
0010    0000000c amsg:      .word msg
                 #==========================================
0014    fedff0ef _start:    jal ra, sub    # execution starts here
0018    00000000            halt
=============================================== Output
Hi
============================================ Program statistics
Input file name       = r0402.a
Instructions executed = 5 (decimal)
Program size          = 1c (hex) 28 (decimal)
Load point            = 0 (hex) 0 (decimal)
Programmer            = Anthony J. Dos Reis
```

Specifies entry point

Entry point

We fixed the bug in the program in r0401.a by changing the label caller to _start. Suppose we want to keep the label caller but still indicate the entry point. We can do this in two ways:

1. We can use both the caller and the _start labels, but they must be on separate lines:

        _start:
        caller: jal ra, sub

    Both labels apply to the jal instruction.

2. We can specify the entry point with the .start directive:

                .start caller   # specifies entry pont
                    ⋮
        caller: jal ra, sub

Warning: Some assemblers do not support the .start directive.

Now consider the following program:

```
address                              r0403.a
0000            lw t0, y     # loads the address of x
0004            halt
0008 x:         .word 10     # translated to the constant 0000000a hex
000c y:         .word x      # translated to 00000008 hex (address of x)
```

The first .word directive is translated to the binary equivalent of 10 decimal. The second .word directive specifies the label x. A label is a symbolic address. Thus, the assembler translates this .word directive to the 32-bit address of x *relative to the beginning of the program*. The assembler does not know what the load point will be when the program is ultimately executed. Thus, it cannot assemble the last line to the address x will ultimately have when the executable form of the program is loaded into memory. The label x is at the address 8 relative to the beginning of the program. Thus, in the machine code in the executable file for this program, the location corresponding to y contains the binary equivalent of 8 hex. Note that this address is the correct address of x *only if* the load point of the program is 0. If, for example, the load point is 300, then the address of x is 308—not 8. Thus, if the load point is nonzero, the rv program (acting as the operation system) has to adjust the location corresponding to y when it loads the program into memory. Specifically, it has to *add* the load point to the location corresponding to y so that it contains the correct address of x.

When the rv program assembles the program in r0403.a, it produces the executable file r0403.e. If we run the program in r0403.e by entering

```
    rv r0403.e -x -m
```

the rv program loads the program starting at location 0. For this load point, no adjustment of the location corresponding to y is required. Thus, when the program ends, 8 (the address of x) will be in t0 as a result of the lw instruction. The -x command line argument causes the registers to be displayed when the program ends so you can confirm that 8 is in t0. The -m command line argument causes memory to be displayed when the program ends so you can confirm that 8 is in the location corresponding to y. But if we load and run the program at location 300 hex by entering

```
    rv r0403.e -L 300 -x -m
```

then at load time, the rv program has to adjust the location in memory corresponding to y. The display of registers and memory confirms that rv does indeed make this adjustment:

```
------------------------------------------------- Memory display
3000:  00c1a283
3004:  00000000        Adjusted
3008:  0000000a        address
300c:  00000308
--------------------------------------------   End of memory display
                                 Adjusted
                                 address
----------------------------------------------- Register display
pc  = 00000308
x0  = 00000000   ra  = 00000000   sp  = 00010000   gp  = 00000300
tp  = 00000000   t0  = 00000308   t1  = 00000000   t2  = 00000000
s0  = 00000000   s1  = 00000000   a0  = 00000000   a1  = 00000000
a2  = 00000000   a3  = 00000000   a4  = 00000000   a5  = 00000000
a6  = 00000000   a7  = 00000000   s2  = 00000000   s3  = 00000000
s4  = 00000000   s5  = 00000000   s6  = 00000000   s7  = 00000000
s8  = 00000000   s9  = 00000000   s10 = 00000000   s11 = 00000000
t3  = 00000000   t4  = 00000000   t5  = 00000000   t6  = 00000000
------------------------------------------------ End of register display
```

If we assemble the following program, we get exactly the same machine code we get for the program in r0403.a. Now, however, the constant 8, not the address of x (which is also 8), is at y.

```
                              r0404.a
1          lw t0, y      # loads the constant 8
2          halt
3 x:       .word 10      # translated to the constant 0000000a hex
4 y:       .word 8       # translated to the constant 00000008 hex
```

When the rv program loads this program into memory, it should *not* adjust the location corresponding to y because it contains a constant—not the address of x. The machine code for this program is *identical* to the machine code for the program in r0403.e. So how does the rv program (acting as the operating system) know to adjust the location corresponding to y in r0403.e (which holds the address of x) but not the location corresponding to y in r0404.e (which holds the constant 8)? The answer is that the header in r0403.e, but *not* the header in r0404.e, has an entry that indicates that the location corresponding to y is an address, and, therefore, should be adjusted according to the load point. Specifically, its header has the following A entry ("A" is for "address"):

A   0000000c

which indicates that at location 000c relative to the beginning of the program is an address. When the rv program at load time detects this entry in the executable file r0403.e, it knows it has to adjust the location at the address 000c relative to the beginning of the program. Thus, if it loads the program into location 300, it has to adjust the address at the location 300 + 000c = 30c. It address this address by adding the load point 300 to the location at 30c. Try assembling both r0403.a and r0404.a and examine the ".1st" files produced (which show the header). In the former, the header contains the A entry above; the latter does not. Thus, for r0404.a, the rv program does not perform any address adjustment.

Assembly Process

To translate an assembly language instruction, an assembler needs to know

- the opcode for the mnemonic
- if the instruction includes any register names, the numbers of those registers
- if the instruction specifies an operand using a label, the address corresponding to that label.

For example, to translate

        lw t0, x

the assembler needs to know the opcode (including the *funct3* and *funct7* fields if used) for the mnemonic lw (*funct3* = 010, *opcode* = 0000011), the register number of t0 (00101), and the address that corresponds to the label x. Opcode and register information can be built into the assembler in the form of a table of the mnemonics and their corresponding opcodes and a similar table for registers:

<table>
<tr><td colspan="2" align="center">Opcode table</td><td colspan="2" align="center">Register table</td></tr>
<tr><td>Opcode</td><td>*funct7/funct3/opcode*</td><td>Name</td><td>Number</td></tr>
<tr><td>lui</td><td>-/-/0110111</td><td>zero</td><td>00000</td></tr>
<tr><td>jal</td><td>-/-/1101111</td><td>ra</td><td>00001</td></tr>
<tr><td>lw</td><td>-/010/0000011</td><td>sp</td><td>00010</td></tr>
<tr><td>add</td><td>0000000/000/0110011</td><td>gp</td><td>00011</td></tr>
<tr><td>⋮</td><td>⋮</td><td>⋮</td><td>⋮</td></tr>
<tr><td></td><td></td><td>x31</td><td>11111</td></tr>
</table>

However, the assembler has to determine the address of each label. It does this in its first pass over the program. During the first pass, it reads each line of the program. If a line starts with a label, the assembler enters that label and its address (relative to the beginning of the program) into a *symbol table*. The assembler starts the first pass by setting a variable named location_counter to 0 and reading the first line of the program. Thus, initially the value of location_counter is the address of the first line of the program. Just before reading the next line, the assembler increments location_counter by the number of memory words required by the first line. Thus, after reading the second line, the value of location_counter is the address of the second line. The assembler continues this process of incrementing location_counter and reading a line so that at any point during the first pass, the value of location_counter is the address of the most recently read line of the program. If that line starts with a label, the assembler enters that label and the value of location_counter (which is the address of that label) into the symbol table. For example, consider the following program:

```
        r0405.a
1 │ # assembling example
2 │          lw t0, x
3 │          dout t0
4 │          halt
5 │ x:       .word 5
```

Line 1 is a comment so it is ignored by the assembler. When the assembler reads the last line of this program, `location_counter` will have the value 12 because it has been incremented (by 4 bytes) three times (once before reading line 3, once before reading line 4, and once before reading line 5). Because line 5 starts with the label x, the assembler enters x and 0...01100 (the value in `location_counter`) into the symbol table. At the conclusion of the first pass, the symbol table contains all the labels in the program and their corresponding addresses. For the program above, we get the following symbol table:

Symbol	Address
x	0...01100

For most lines during the first pass, the assembler increments `location_counter` by 4 because most lines of an assembly language program are translated to a single word of machine code. However, for the `.asciz` and `.string` directives, the assembler has to increment `location_counter` by the length of the string (including the null character at the end). Similarly, for the `.zero` and `.space` directives, the assembler has to increment `location_counter` by the number of bytes in the block. For a line that is blank or that contains only a comment or a label, the assembler does not increment `location_counter`.

During the second pass, the assembler again reads the program and maintains `location_counter` so that it holds the address of each line during its processing as it did during the first pass. For each instruction, the assembler determines the binary for its various parts by looking up those parts in its opcode, register, and symbol tables. It then "assembles" those component parts into a 32-bit machine instruction. For example, for the `lw` instruction in `r0405.a`, the assembler looks up the opcode for `lw` in the opcode table, the register number of `t0` in the register table, and the address of x in the symbol table. It assembles the parts (along with the number of the gp register for the *rs1* field) into the corresponding 32-bit machine instruction:

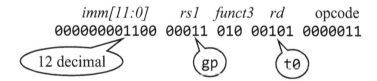

To assemble a `jal` instruction is a little more complicated than assembling a `lw` instruction because a `jal` instruction uses a `pc`-relative address. For example, consider the following program:

```
          r0406.a
1 │ # deterimining relative address
2 │          addi t0, x0, 5
3 │          jal ra, sub
4 │          halt
5 │ sub:     dout t0
6 │          jalr x0, 0(ra)
```

Recall that a pc-relative address of a label in an instruction is the label's address relative to the address in the pc register when that instruction is being fetched. The address in the pc register when the instruction is being fetched is, of course, just the address of that instruction. Thus, the pc-relative address is the difference of the address of the label and the address of the instruction. The value of location_counter is 4 when the assembler is processing the jal instruction. The address of sub is 12. Thus, the pc-relative address of sub is given by

(address of sub from symbol table) – (location_counter when processing jal) = 12 – 4 = 8

After computing the pc-relative address, the assembler assembles it (after permuting its bits as required by the jal instruction), the number of the destination register, and the opcode into the machine instruction:

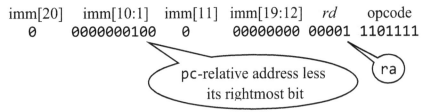

imm[20]	imm[10:1]	imm[11]	imm[19:12]	rd	opcode
0	0000000100	0	00000000	00001	1101111

Recall that the jump-to address always has a 0 in its rightmost bit. Thus, this 0 bit does is not stored in the machine instruction. The immediate value in the instruction above, with its bits in the proper order, is equal to 0...0100. With the omitted 0 bit added on its right end, we get 0...01000 (8 decimal), the pc-relative address of sub.

An assembler is so called because its principal activity is to assemble (i.e., put together) the machine instructions from its component parts.

Current Location Marker

If an asterisk appears in place of a label in an assembly language, the asterisk represents the current location in the program. For example, consider the following program,

```
                              r0407.a
1          lw  t0, amsg        # get address of msg
2          sout t0             # prompt user
3          din t0              # read in a negative or non-negative number
4          blt t0, x0, *+12    # branch on negative to hout instruction
5          dout t0             # display non-negative number in decimal
6          beq x0, x0, *+8     # unconditional branch to halt instruction
7          hout t0             # display negative number in hex
8          halt
9  amsg:   .word msg
10 msg:    .asciz "Enter decimal number\n"
```

The asterisk in the blt instruction represents the location of the blt instruction. Thus, "*+12" is the address of the hout instruction. Similarly, the asterisk in the beq instruction represents the location of that instruction. Thus, "*+8" represents the address of the halt instruction. This program displays negative numbers in hex, and non-negative numbers in decimal.

.data and .text Sections

A program can be divided into two parts: a .text section and a .data section. The .text section contains the program's instructions, and the .data section, the program's data. If no section directive appears in a program, the entire program defaults to a .text section.

On most systems (but not on rv), the .text section is read-only. Thus, any attempt to store into the .text section would immediately produce an error message ("Segmentation error" or "Program stopped running"), and terminate the program. Because a .text section typically is read-only, read/write data cannot be in a .text section. However, read-only data (i.e., constants) can be in a .text section in addition to instructions.

In all the programs we have seen so far, the gp register is initialized with the load point of the program. However, if a program has a .data section, then the gp register is initialized with the address of the *middle* of the .data section. Initializing gp with the address of the middle of the .data section allows a load or store instruction to take advantage of the negative offsets it can specify (−2048 to −1) as well as the non-negative offsets (0 to +2047). Thus, a load or store instruction can access up to 4096 bytes of data—2048 bytes in either direction from the base address in the gp register. If, however, the gp register were initialized to the address of the *beginning* of the .data section, a load or store instruction then could use only non-negative offsets to access data (because there would be no data at negative offsets). Thus, a load or store instruction would be able to access at most 2048 bytes of data.

If a program has a .text directive, the pc register is initialized so that it points to the start of the .text directive unless the program specifies an entry point (with either the .start directive or the _start label). If the program specifies an entry point, then the pc register is initialized to the specified entry point.

The following program has a .data section. Thus, the gp register is initialized to point to the middle of the .data section (to the location corresponding to the label sum). Thus, the labels that precede sum have negative offsets, the labels that follow have positive offsets, and sum has a 0 offset.

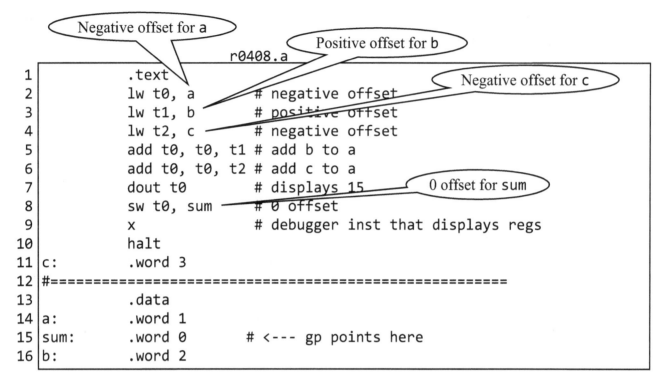

There are several advantages in using a `.text` section and a `.data` section:

1. Separating data from instructions allows data and instructions to be stored in separate memory modules. Instructions and data can then be fetched simultaneously (because they are in different modules). Faster execution of instructions may then be possible.

2. Without a `.data` section, the range of the load and store instructions include instructions as well as data (unless all the data is at the beginning of the program). Thus, without a `.data` section, less data can be accessed by the load and store instructions.

3. If the `.text` section is read-only (which is usually the case), any attempt to store over an instruction is immediately detected.

4. By separating data from instructions, multiple users can share a single copy of a read-only `.text` section.

Note: Some assemblers support three distinct data-type sections: `.data` (for read/write data), `.bss` (for uninitialized read/write data), and `.rodata` (for read-only data). The `rv` program, however, treats all three the same way (as a read/write `.data` section). Moreover, `rv` does not supports sections with multiple parts. For example, a `.data` section followed by a `.text` section followed by a continuation of the `.data` section is not supported.

PseudoInstructions

The prefix "pseudo" means "not real". Thus, a *pseudoinstruction* is not a real instruction. For example, the RISC-V has a `blt` instruction but not a `bgt` instruction. Nevertheless, in an assembly language program, we can use the `bgt` mnemonic. For example, the following instruction is legal (assuming "`done`" appears as a label on some line in the program):

```
bgt t0, t1, done
```

Given that there is no `bgt` instruction (i.e., there is no opcode that corresponds to this mnemonic), how can this be a legal instruction? Note that the contents of `t0` is greater than the contents of `t1` if and only if the contents of `t1` is less than the contents of `t0`. Thus, the following `blt` instruction (which is a real instruction) does precisely what the `bgt` instruction above is supposed to do (i.e., branch if `t0` is greater than `t1`):

```
blt t1, t0, done
```

So the assembler translates the fake `bgt` instruction above to the machine language for the `blt` instruction.
   Here are all the branching pseudoinstructions that are like `bgt`:

`bgt` *rs1, rs2, label*	(branch greater than)
`ble` *rs1, rs2, label*	(branch less than or equal)
`bgtu` *rs1, rs2, label*	(branch greater than unsigned)
`bleu` *rs2, rs2, label*	(branch less than or equal unsigned)

The instruction

```
beq t0, x0, done
```

branches if the contents of `t0` and `x0` are equal. Because `x0` contains 0, the instruction branches if `t0` is 0. The equivalent pseudoinstruction is

```
beqz t0, done
```

Using this pseudoinstruction saves us from having to specify `x0` as the register to use in the comparison with the register we do specify (`t0` in this example). Here are all the branching pseudoinstructions like `beqz` that compare the *rs1* register with `x0` (the *rs2* field is set to 00000—the register number of the `x0` register).

`beqz` *rs1, label*	(branch if *rs1* equal zero)
`bnez` *rs1, label*	(branch if *rs1* not equal zero)
`bltz` *rs1, label*	(branch if *rs1* less than zero)
`bgez` *rs1, label*	(branch if *rs1* greater than or equal zero
`bgtz` *rs1, label*	(branch if *rs1* greater than zero)
`blez` *rs1, label*	(branch if *rs1* less than or equal zero)

The pseudoinstructions that test if a register's contents are zero or nonzero, respectively, are `seqz` and `snez`:

`seqz` *rd, rs1*	(set if *rs1* equal to 0)
`snez` *rd, rs1*	(set if *rs1* not equal to 0)

For example,

```
seqz t0, t1
```

sets t0 to 1 if t1 is zero. Otherwise, it sets t0 to 0. It is translated to the machine language for

```
sltiu t0, t1, 1
```

The pseudoinstruction

```
snez t0, t1
```

sets t0 to 1 if t0 is nonzero. Otherwise, it sets t0 to 0. It is translated to the machine language for

```
sltu t0, x0, t1
```

The pseudo instructions

```
sltz rd, rs1  (set if rs1 less than zero)
sgtz rd, rs1  (set if rs1 is greater than zero)
```

are also translated to set-compare instructions. They set the *rd* register to 1 if the *rs1* register is less 0 or greater than 0, respectively.

The pseudoinstructions j and jr are translated to the jal and jalr instructions, respectively. For both the j and jr instructions, the *rd* field is set to 00000 (the number of the x0 register). Thus, the instructions jump but do not save a return address (because x0 is permanently set to 0). The instruction

```
j label
```

is translated to the machine language for

```
jal x0, label
```

The instruction,

```
jr rs1
```

is translated to the machine language for

```
jalr x0, 0(rs1)
```

The ret pseudoinstruction is translated to the machine language for

```
jalr x0, 0(ra)
```

Thus, it jumps to the address in the ra register, but it does not save a return address. Use this pseudoinstruction at the end of a subroutine to return to its caller.

Here is a list of some more pseudoinstuctions, along with the real instruction to which they are translated:

Pseudo instruction	Translated to	Effect
mv *rd, rs1*	addi *rd, rs1,* 0	Moves the contents of *rs1* reg to *rd* reg
neg *rd, rs1*	sub *rd,* x0, *rs1*	Negates copy of *rs1* reg, loads *rd* reg with result
not *rd, rs1*	xori *rd, rs1,* -1	Flips bits in copy of *rs1* reg, loads *rd* reg with result
nop	addi x0, x0, 0	No operation

The li (load immediate) instruction loads a constant into the *rd* register. For example, the following two li instructions load −5 and 20000 into the t0 and t1 registers:

```
li t0, -5
li t1, 20000
```

The li pseudoinstruction can load any 32-bit number into the *rd* register. If the number can fit in the 12-bit immediate value field of an addi instruction, then the li instruction is translated to just an addi instruction. But it the number is too big for the immediate value field, then the li instruction is translated to a lui-addi sequence. The lui instruction loads the *rd* register with the upper 20 bits of the number; the addi then loads the lower 12 bits. Here is the assembly listing of several li instructions:

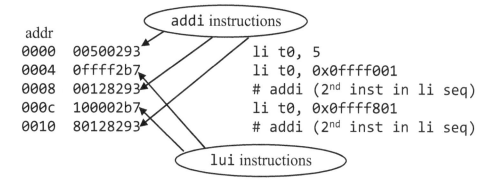

```
addr
0000    00500293            li t0, 5
0004    0ffff2b7            li t0, 0x0ffff001
0008    00128293            # addi (2nd inst in li seq)
000c    100002b7            li t0, 0x0ffff801
0010    80128293            # addi (2nd inst in li seq)
```

The number in the first li instruction can fit in the immediate value field of an addi instruction. Thus, it is translated to just the addi instruction, 00500293, at the address 0000 (the immediate value is in its upper three hex digits). The number in the second li instruction is too big for the immediate value field of an addi instruction. Thus, it is translated to a lui instruction at the address 0004 followed by an addi instruction at the address 0008. The upper five hex digits (0ffff) in the lui instruction at address 0004 are the upper 20 bits of the number to be loaded. The upper three hex digits (001) in the addi instruction are the lower 12 bits of the number to be loaded.

Before we examine the last li instruction above, you need to know the answer to the following question: If you add a binary number of all 1's to a number *x*, and then add 1, what do you get? The answer is *x*. All 1's represents −1 (recall the two's complement of +1 is all 1's). If you add all 1's (i.e., −1) to *x* and then add 1, the two additions cancel each other out. Thus, you get back *x*.

Now let's get back to the last li instruction above, which is translated to a lui-addi sequence because the number to be loaded (0x0ffff801) is too big to fit into the immediate value field of an addi instruction. The immediate value in the addi instruction at address 0010 is 801 hex. The lui instruction at address 000c zeros out the lower 12 bits of the destination register t0. Thus, when the immediate value in the `addi` instruction is added to `t0`, the lower 12 bits of `t0` become the binary equivalent of 801 hex. But recall that the immediate value in an `addi` instruction is a *signed* number. Thus, it is sign extended. Because the leftmost bit in the binary representation of the immediate value 801 hex is 1, it is sign extended with 1's, the effect of the `addi` is not only to set the lower 12 bits of `t0` to 801 hex (*as it should*), but also to add all 1's (that come from the sign extension) to the upper 20 bits of `t0` (*as it should NOT!*). To compensate for the 1's from the sign extension, the immediate value loaded by the `lui` instruction is one more that the upper 20 bits of the constants specified by the `li` assembly language instruction. Note that at address 000c, the upper 20 bits of the constant in the assembly language instruction in hex are 0x0ffff, but the immediate value in the `lui` machine instruction (its upper 5 hex digits) is 0x10000, which is one more than 0x0ffff. The added 1 cancels out the 1's from the sign extension that are added to the upper 20 bits by the `addi` instruction. The result is that the destination register receives the correct value.

The `la` (load address) pseudoinstruction loads the address of the specified label into the destination register. For example, the following instruction loads `t0` with the address of `msg`:

```
la t0, msg  # load address of msg into t0
```

It is translated into an `auipc-addi` sequence. The `auipc` instruction loads `t0` with the upper 20-bits of the address of the label. The `addi` instruction loads the lower 12 bits. Like the `lui` instruction in the expansion of the `li` pseudoinstruction, the immediate value in the `auipc` instruction is one more that the upper 20 bits of the address of the specified label if the leftmost bit in the immediate value of the `addi` instruction is 1 to compensate for the sign extension of the immediate value in the `addi` instruction.

The only difference in effect between the `lui` and `auipc` instructions is that the `auipc` instruction *also* adds the current address in the `pc` register to the destination register. Thus, the immediate values in the `auipc` and `addi` instruction should provide only the `pc`-relative address of the label. Then because the `auipc` instruction also adds the address in the `pc` register, the destination register receives the 32-bit absolute address of the specified label. Sounds complicated, and it is. But the assembler does the address computation for us.

To get the address of a string, we have been using a `lw` instruction in combination with a `.word` directive that provides the address of the string. For example,

```
        lw t0, amsg
        sout t0
          ⋮
amsg:   .word msg
msg:    .asciz "Enter decimal number\n"
```

Now with the `la` pseudoinstruction, we can do this instead:

```
        la t0, msg
        sout t0
          ⋮
msg:    .asciz "Enter decimal number\n"
```

The mnemonics for all the instructions whose third operand is an immediate value end in the letter "i". For example, the third operand in an `addi` instruction should be an immediate value. Suppose we forget to include the letter "i" in the mnemonic. For example, suppose we write the instruction

```
add t0, t0, 1
```

The `add` instruction should have three operands, all registers. So you would think that this is an illegal `add` instruction. But because the third operand is an immediate value, the assembler translates it as if the mnemonic were `addi`. The `sub`, `sll`, `slt`, `sltu`, `xor`, `srl`, `sra`, `or`, and `and` mnemonics are "corrected" in the same way if they are specified with an immediate value in place of a register.

The `jal` and `jalr` instruction are also "corrected" if the register to receive the return address is not specified in the assembly language instruction. If this is the case, the assembler translates them as if the `ra` register were specified. For example, the `jal` instruction,

```
jal sub
```

is translated as if it were

```
jal ra, sub
```

The use of pseudoinstructions can make writing and reading programs easier. For example,

```
mv t0, t1
```

is certainly clearer that the equivalent

```
addi t0, t1, 0
```

The downside of pseudoinstructions is that they require you to learn more mnemonics, and some do not make a program more readable. Moreover, their use can obscure the actual instruction set of a computer. When you are first learning the instruction set of a computer, it might be a good idea to avoid pseudoinstructions. Alternatively, you might confine your use of pseudoinstructions to the following few, all of which do make a program more readable: `j`, `la`, `li`, `mv`, `not`, `neg`, `ret`, `seqz`, and `snez`.

Variations on Instruction Formats

In an assembly language program, a label operand in an instruction can be followed by a plus or minus sign and a constant. For example, the following instructions are all legal:

```
lw t0, x+8          # load second word after x
sw t0, x-4          # store word just before x
beq x0, x0, xyz-8   # branch to two insts before xyz inst
jal ra, xyz+4       # jump to inst that follows xyz inst
jal ra, xyz-8       # jump to two insts before xyz inst
```

For all these instructions, the assembler gets the address of the label from the symbol table. It then adjusts that address according the constant, if any. For example, for the operand x+8, the assembler gets the address of x, and then adds 8 to it. It then assembles the resulting address into the machine instruction.

A .word directive can have a label operand, in which case the operand is translated to a word that contains the address of the label. As in instructions with label operands, a label operand in a .word directive can be followed by a plus or minus sign and a constant. For example, the following .word directive defines two words. The first contains the address of x. The second contains the address of the address of x plus 4:

```
.word x, x+4
```

Another variation in instruction format that is legal—although not used very often—is to have just a constant in place of operand with the label. We mention this variation only because you may see code that uses it in other books on the RISC-V. Here are some examples:

```
lw t0, 8
beq x0, x0, 12
jal ra, 4
```

The assembler translates the constant in these instructions the same way it would translate the instruction with a label whose address is the specified constant. For example, in the following program, the address of x is 8. If we replace 8 in the lw instruction with x, we get an instruction that is translated to the same machine language instruction as the original:

```
        lw t0, 8    # equivalent to lw t0, x
        halt
x:      .word 5     # address of x is 8
```

For both versions of the lw instruction, its immediate value field contains 8, and its *rs1* field contains the number of the gp register. Thus, both instructions load from the location whose address is the address in the gp register plus 8.

Problems

1. Which is better: a la instruction or a lw instruction in combination with a .word directive that provides the address of a label?

2. Translate to machine language. Give your answers in hex:

```
        beq t4, sp, *
        beq ra, gp, *+4
        beq s0, x31, *-4
        ret
```

3. Write a single instruction that loads its address into t0.

4. Why is the immediate value in a load or store instruction a signed number? What advantages would accrue if it were an unsigned number? *Hint*: Consider a stack frame.

5. Run a program with rv. Specify the -d command line switch when you invoke rv. As soon as the debugger displays its prompt, enter

```
m c000 10
```

which displays 10 words starting at location c000 hex. What is there?

6. Does the following li instruction generate a single addi instruction or a two-instruction sequence:

```
li t0, 0xfffffffc
```

7. Explain what happens and why it happens when the following program is executed:

```
loop:      addi sp, sp, -4
           sw t0, 0(sp)
           beq x0, x0, loop
```

8. What would be the effect of adding 4 to the gp register during program execution.

9. How does rv respond if a program includes both the _start label and a .start directive?

10. Suppose you wanted to call a subroutine via its starting label that was out of the range of the jal instruction. How would you do it? Suppose you want to load a value from a label that was out of the range of the lw instruction. How would you do it?

11. Give a two-instruction sequence that can jump to any 32-bit absolute halfword address without using a .word directive that provides the address. *Hint*: The jump-to address in a jalr instruction is given by the contents of the *rs1* register plus the immediate value in the instruction.

12. Assemble by hand the following program. Give your answer in hex. *After* assembling it yourself, check your answers by assembling the program with rv.

```
           snez t0, t1
           ble t0, a0, done+4
           li t1, 0xffff800
           la t1, x
done:      halt
sub:       ret
           .data
           .space 4, 7
           .zero 4
x:         .word 5
```

13. What is the effect of the instructions in the program below on the contents of t0 and t1? Use the c debugger command to initialize the t0 and t1 registers with 1 and 2, respectively. Then step though the instructions with the debugger to see what happens.

```
xor t0, t0, t1
xor t1, t0, t1
xor t0, t0, t1
halt
```

14. Why was RISC-V designed so that the load and store instructions do not use pc-relative addressing?

15. How does rv know what to initialize the gp register to if the program has a .data section? How does rv know what to initialize the pc register to if the program has a .text section but does not specify an entry point? *Hint*: Look at the ".lst" files for such programs.

16. What is in the header for the following program:

```
x:          .word x
y:          .word x
_start:     halt
```

17. Write and run an assembly language program that reads in 10 integers, sorts them into ascending order, and displays the sorted numbers.

18. Write and run an assembly language program that reads in a string, stores its successive characters on the stack, then pops the stack, displaying each character as it is popped, all on the same line. Thus, the inputted string should be displayed in reverse order

19. Write and run an assembly language program whose top level calls sub1. sub1 reads in a positive integer and calls sub2, passing it the inputted integer in a0. sub2 computes the nth Fibonacci number, returning it to sub1 via a0. sub1 then returns to the top level, returning the Fibonacci number via a0. Finally, the top level displays the Fibonacci number it receives from sub1. Test your program using 0, 1, 2, and 50 as inputs. *Note*: $Fib_1 = 1$, $Fib_2 = 1$, $Fib_n = Fib_{n-1} + Fig_{n-2}$ for $n > 2$.

20. Write and run an assembly language program in which the top level reserves two words on the stack, inputs two positive integers and pushes them of the stack (below the two reserved words), and then calls sub. sub should divide the first number pushed on the stack by the second number. It should put the quotient in the first word on the stack reserved by the top level, and the remainder in the second reserved word, and then return to the top level. The top level should then pop the top two words on the stack (the inputted numbers) to discard them, then pop and display the quotient and remainder. To determine the quotient and the remainder, do not use the div and rem instructions. Instead, subtract repeatedly the divisor from the dividend until the dividend becomes negative. Then add the divisor once to the dividend. The quotient is the (number of subtractions) – 1. The remainder is the final value of the dividend.

5 Multiplication and Division

Shift-Add Algorithm

The RV32I base instruction set does not have a multiply instruction. We can, nevertheless, multiply on a computer that supports only RV32I. One simple way to multiply is to repeatedly add the number that is multiplied. For example, to multiply 7 by 5, simply add up five 7's. Although this procedure gives us the correct answer, it requires many additions if the multiplier is large, and therefore can be very inefficient.

The second approach to multiplication is to use a loop that repeatedly performs shift and add operations. We call this approach the *shift-add algorithm* (an *algorithm* is a procedure that solves a problem in a finite number of steps). The shift-add algorithm does multiplication in essentially the same way we do multiplication with a pencil and paper. Let's look at some examples. To keep our discussion simple, we will use binary numbers that are only four bits wide (thus, they can range from −8 to 7).

Let's multiply the binary numbers 0010 (2 decimal) by 0011 (3 decimal). We call the number we are multiplying by the *multiplier* (0011 in this example) and the multiplied number (0010 in this example) the *multiplicand*.

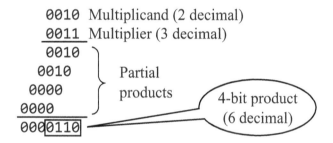

We multiply the multiplicand by each bit in the multiplier starting with the rightmost bit in the multiplier. Each one of these multiplications results in a partial product. We do not really need to multiply to determine the partial products: If the bit in the multiplier is 0, the partial product is 0; if the bit is 1, the partial product is equal to the multiplicand. The right bit of each partial product is positioned in the same column as the multiplier bit that produced it. For example, when the multiplicand is multiplied by the second bit from the right in the multiplier, the partial product produced is positioned so that its rightmost bit is positioned in the same column as the second bit of the multiplier. To compute the final product, the partial products are added. The four rightmost bits of the sum is the product.

With the shift-add algorithm, both the multiplicand and multiplier can be positive, negative, or zero. The only restriction is that the product has to fit into the same number of bits that are in the multiplicand and multiplier (four bits in our example). For example, here is the multiplication of 1111 by 1111 (recall that 1111 equals −1):

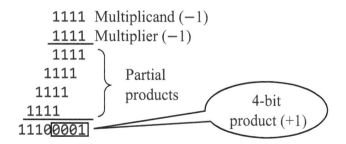

The rightmost four bits of the sum of the partial products is the final product (+1).

Here is the pseudocode for the shift-add algorithm:

Set `product` to 0.
While (`multiplier` not equal to 0)
{
    If (rightmost bit of `multiplier` is equal to 1)
        add `multiplicand` to `product`.
    Left shift `multiplicand` one position.
    Right shift `multiplier` one position.
}

Each time through the loop, we shift `multiplicand` one position to the left so that whenever it is added to `product`, it is in the correct position. In addition, each time through the loop, we shift `multiplier` one position to the right so that each time through the loop the next bit in `multiplier` is in the rightmost position, and therefore easy to test.

Multiplying with Software

Let's implement the shift-add algorithm in RISC-V assembly language. We will use `t0` to accumulate the sum of the partial products. Note that the partial products produced for each 1-bit in the multiplier are all equal to the appropriately shifted multiplicand. Thus, for each 1-bit in the multiplier, we add the appropriately shifted multiplicand to `t0`. At the conclusion of this procedure, `t0` will have the product.

Here is a program that reads in two integers, passes them in `a0` and `a1` to the `shiftadd` subroutine. The `shiftadd` subroutine multiplies the two numbers it is passed using the shift-add algorithm, and passes the product back to the caller via `a0`. The caller code then displays the product. Note that we are using some pseudoinstructions in this program: `li` (load immediate) on line 6, `j` (unconditional jump) on line 13, `mv` (move) on line 14, `ret` (return) on line 14, and `la` on lines 17 and 23.

r0501.a

```
 1 # multiplication using the shift-add algorithm
 2 # a0 is multiplicand
 3 # a1 is multiplier
 4 # t0 is product
 5           .text
 6 shiftadd: li t0, 0          # set product to 0
 7 loop:     beq a1, x0, done  # test if multiplier is 0
 8           andi t1, a1, 1    # test rightmost bit of multiplier
 9           beq t1, x0, noadd # branch if multiplier bit is 0
10           add t0, t0, a0    # add multiplicand to product
11 noadd:    slli a0, a0, 1    # shift multiplicand left
12           srli a1, a1, 1    # shift multiplier right
13           j loop            # do loop again
14  done:    mv a0, t0         # copy product to a0
15           ret               # return to caller
16 #==================================================
17 _start:   la t0, prompt     # get address of prompt message
18           sout t0           # prompt the user
19           din a0            # input multiplicand
20           sout t0           # prompt the user
21           din a1            # input multiplier
22           jal ra, shiftadd  # call multipy subroutine
23           la t0, msg        # get address of msg
24           sout t0           # display "Product = "
25           dout a0           # display product
26           nl                # move cursor to start of next line
27           halt
28 #============================================================
29           .data
30 prompt:   .asciz "Enter decimal integer: "
31 msg:      .asciz "Product = "
```

RV32M Standard Extension and Doubleword Support

The rv program supports both the RV32I base instruction set and the RV32M standard extension. The RV32M extension provides the following 32-bit multiply, division, and remainder instructions:

mul (multiply)
mulh (multiply high)
mulhsu (multiply high signed unsigned)
mulhu (multiply high unsigned)
div (divide)
divu (divide unsigned)
rem (remainder)
remu (remainder unsigned)

Obviously, if your computer supports RV32M, then you would use its multiply instructions to multiply—not the shift-add algorithm.

To get the 32-bit product of two 32-bit numbers, use the `mul` instruction. For example, to multiply the contents of `t1` and `t2` and put the product in `t0`, use

```
mul t0, t1, t2    # product of t1 and t2 goes into t0
```

However, when multiplying two *n*-bit numbers, the product can require up to $2 \times n$ bits. For example, the product of the *two*-bit unsigned numbers, 11 and 11 (3 and 3 decimal), is the *four*-bit number 1001 (9 decimal). Thus, when multiplying two 32-bit numbers, the product may require 64 bits. The `mul` instruction provides the lower 32 bits of the product (for both signed and unsigned numbers); the `mulh` instruction (for signed numbers) and the `mulhu` instruction (for unsigned numbers) provide the upper 32 bits of the product. For example, suppose the numbers in `t2` and `t3` are signed numbers. To get their 64-bit product, use

```
mul t0, t2, t3    # lower 32 bits of product goes into t0
mulh t1, t2, t3   # upper 32 bits of product goes into t1
```

If the numbers in `t2` and `t3` and unsigned, then use

```
mul t0, t2, t3    # lower 32 bits of product goes into t0
mulhu t1, t2, t3  # upper 32 bits of product goes into t1
```

The `mulhsu` instruction provides the upper 32 bits of a mixed multiplication (i.e., signed number × unsigned number).

The `div` and `divu` are the division instructions for signed and unsigned numbers, respectively. `rem` and `remu` are the remainder instructions for signed and unsigned numbers, respectively. For example, to divide the signed number in `t1` by the signed number in `t2`, use

```
div t0, t1, t2    # quotient goes into t0
```

Use the `ddout` (doubleword decimal out) instruction to display a signed doubleword in decimal. Use the `dudout` (double unsigned out) instruction to display an unsigned doubleword in decimal. Use `dhout` (double hex out) to display a doubleword in hex. All three instructions display the doubleword in any two "adjacent" registers. Two registers are adjacent if they are next to each other in the circular list consisting of the registers `x5` though `x31`:

```
x5, x6, ..., x31        Circular list: x5 follows x31.
```

For example, `x5-x6`, `x31-x5`, and `t1-t2` are adjacent pairs, but not `t2-t3` (because `t2` is `x7`, and `t3` is `x28`). The register specified by the doubleword output instructions is the first register in the pair. For example, the instruction

```
ddout t0
```

displays the doubleword in the `t0-t1` pair. Prior to the execution of this `ddout` instruction, `t0` should be loaded with the low-order word of the doubleword to be displayed, and `t1` should be loaded with the high-order word.

The following program displays the doubleword at `x` in both hex (using `dhout`) and in decimal (using `ddout`). The `.dword` directive creates a doubleword constant. The operands specified by a `.dword` directive can be decimal, hex, binary, or character constants, but not labels.

```
                              r0502.a
1            lw t0, x           # load t0 with low-order word
2            lw t1, x+4         # load t1 with high-order word
3            dhout t0           # display doubleword in t0-t1 in hex
4            nl                 # move cursor to next line
5            ddout t0           # display doubleword in t0-t1 in decimal
6            halt
7  x:        .dword 0x7fffffffffffffff
```

The program displays

```
7fffffffffffffff
9223372036854775807
```

Problems

1) Write and run an assembly language program that reads in a non-negative integer, computes the factorial of that number, and displays the result. *n* factorial for *n* > 0 is the product of the integers from 1 to *n*. 0 factorial by definition is 1. Use the shift-add algorithm to multiply. Assume the factorial can fit into 32 bits. Test your program with 5.

2) Same as problem 1, but use the `mul` instruction. Assume the factorial can fit into 32 bits. What is the largest factorial that can fit into 32 bits?

3) Write and run an assembly language program that computes and displays 50 factorial. 50 factorial is too big to fit into two registers. Thus, to compute it, you should represent a factorial with a sequence of words in memory, with each word holding just a single digit of the factorial. A sequence of 100 words can hold values up to $10^{100} - 1 = 99...9$ (i.e., one hundred 9-digits). Initialize the 100-word sequence to the value 1. Then multiply it by 2, 3, ... 50. To multiply by 2, multiply each word in the 100-word sequence by 2. To multiply by 3, multiply each word in the 100-word sequence by 3, and so on. After each word in the 100-word sequence is multiplied by the current multiplier, propagate carries so that each word continues to hold just a single digit. For example, after computing 4 factorial, the first word will contain 24. Reset it to its right digit (4) and add the left digit (2) to the next word to the left. To isolate the digits of a multiple-digit decimal number (like 24), you will need to determine the quotient and remainder on a division by 10. For example, if 24 is divided by 10, the remainder is 4 (which is the right digit) and the quotient is the left digit (or digits for numbers with more than two digits).

4) Using an assembly language program, determine the decimal value of 0x876654321.

5) Using an assembly language program, determine the hex value of 3333333333333333333 decimal.

6) Write and run an assembly language program that reads in a decimal number whose rightmost digit is not 0. Multiply repeatedly by 5 ten times. How many trailing zeros are in the final product? Try your program with 2, 3, 4, 5, 6, 7, 8, 64, 512 and 513. Can you predict which numbers will produce a result that has exactly five trailing zeros?

7) Write a program that includes a subroutine that computes powers. Specifically, given an integer n and a positive integer m, your subroutine should compute and return to the caller n^m. Use your program to compute 3^{13}.

8) Write and run an assembly language program that plays the game of Nim. Start with 20 sticks. Human and computer alternate moves. Human goes first. On each move, the human removes 1, 2, or 3 sticks. On each move, computer removes 1, 2, or 3 sticks so that the number of sticks remaining is one more than a multiple of 4. If the number of sticks is already one more than a multiple of 4, then the computer removes one stick. Play continues until the number of sticks goes to zero or goes negative. The player who picks up the last stick loses.

9) Rewrite the program in `r0501.a`, replacing register names with meaningful names.

10) Write a program that lists all the amicable numbers in the interval 1 to 1000. An amicable number is a number equal to the sum of its positive divisors, excluding itself. For example, 6 is an amicable number because the sum of its positive divisors excluding itself (1, 2, and 3) is equal to 6.

11) Write a program that reads in a positive integer and determines if it is *prime* (i.e., if it is greater than 1 and its only positive divisors are 1 and itself).

12) Give the assembly language code that determines if the product of two unsigned 32-bit numbers overflows 32 bits.

13) Same as the preceding problem but for signed numbers.

14) If the product of two n-bit *signed* numbers requires more than n bits, will the shift-add algorithm correctly determine all the bits in the product? Demonstrate your conclusion with some examples.

15) If the product of two n-bit unsigned numbers requires more than n bits, will the shift-add algorithm correctly determine all the bits in the product. Demonstrate your conclusion with some examples.

16) What is the maximum number of times the loop iterates that computes a product by repeatedly adding?

17) What is the maximum number of times the loop iterates in the shift-add algorithm?

18) Is there an algorithm comparable to the shift-add algorithm for division?

19) Why does RV32I have add instructions but not multiply and division instructions?

20) What happens if a program `rv` runs divides by zero? Write and run such a program. Display the computer result, if any, with `dout`.

6 Linking

Separate Assembly

Suppose we want to write a large assembly language program. One approach is to create a single large file containing the entire program. A better approach, however, is to create multiple files each containing the source code for only a single function or for, at most, a collection of closely related functions. We call these modules *source modules* because they hold the source code for the program. To create an executable file from the source modules requires two steps: First, we have to assemble each source module. Each assembly produces an output file called an *object module*:

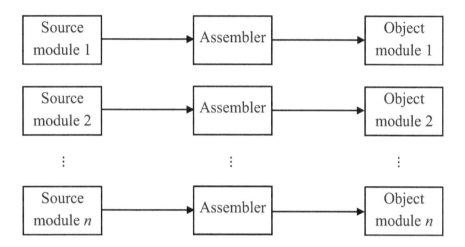

Second, we have to combine all the object modules into a single *executable file*. The program that performs this operation is called a *linker*:

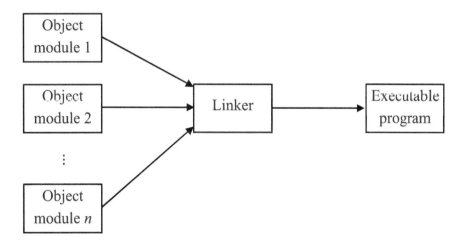

The executable program produced by the linker is sometimes called a *load module* because it is the form of the program that is ready to be loaded into memory by the operating system and executed. By convention, we use the ".a", ".o", and ".e" extensions respectively for the assembly language source module files, the object module files, and the executable program file.

Compilers for the UNIX system and UNIX-like systems (for example, Linux and Raspbian) generate object and executable files in the *Executable and Linkable Format* (ELF). However, the linking mechanism in the `rv` program uses a different format—a much simpler format (ELF is much too complicated for an introduction to linking). Once you understand the linking mechanism that the `rv` program uses, you will be adequately prepared to master more complex formats such as ELF. A limitation of the linker in the `rv` program (which does not negatively impact our investigation of linking) is that it cannot link modules that contains `.data`, `.bss`, or `.rodata` directives.

Requirements for Linking

Let's create a program from two separately-assembled modules—`m1.a`, and `m2.a`—which together constitute a single program. Here are the preliminary versions of these modules:

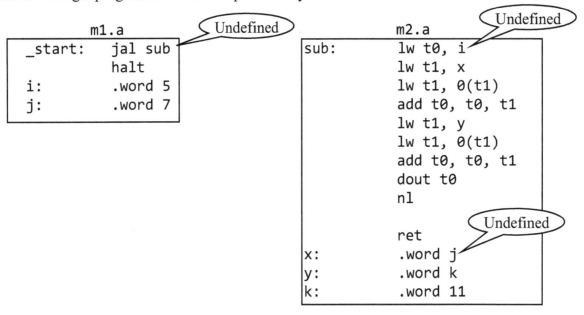

Unfortunately, neither of these modules will assemble correctly. `sub` is an undefined label in `m1.a`. The label `sub` is in `m2.a`, but when the assembler is assembling `m1.a`, it has no knowledge of `m2.a`. Similarly, `i` and `j` in `m2.a` are undefined labels. To allow these modules to assemble, we have to tell the assembler that the undefined labels are *external references*—that is, references to labels that appears in another module. If we do that, then the assembler will assemble the instructions with the external references, placing 0 in their address fields. Then at link time, the linker replaces the 0 in their address fields with the correct addresses. We call this process of adjusting address fields corresponding to external references *resolving external references*.

We tell the assembler that a label is external with an `.extern` directive. For example, in `m1.a`, we need an `.extern` directive for `sub`:

```
        .extern sub         # indicates sub is a label in another module
_start: jal sub
        halt
i:      .word 5
j:      .word 7
```

In m2.a, we need .extern directives for i and j. With these modifications, m1.a, and m2.a will both assemble without error. To assemble, enter

rv m1.a   (Creates m1.o object module)
rv m2.a   (Creates m2.o object module)

Because m1.a and m2.a individually are not complete programs, each assembly above produces an object file (a file with the extension ".o" rather than an executable file). We can then link the two object modules—m1.o, and m2.o—produced by the assembler with the linker in the rv program by entering on the command line

    rv m1.o m2.o

But we then get the following link-time error message:

    sub is an undefined external reference

The problem is that *labels by default are local to the file in which they appear.* Thus, they cannot be referenced from outside that file. For the link to work, we have to make the following labels global: i, and j (in m1.a) and sub (in m2.a). We do this with .global directives. Here are the final versions of m1.a and m2.a with the .global directives included:

m1.a

```
1            .extern sub
2            .global i
3            .global j
4
5 _start:    jal sub
6            halt
7 i:         .word 5
8 j:         .word 7
```

m2.a

```
1             .extern i
2             .extern j
3             .global sub
4
5  sub:       lw t0, i          # get i
6             lw t1, x          # get addr in x
7             lw t1, 0(t1)      # get j
8             add t0, t0, t1    # add j
9             lw t1, y          # get addr in y
10            lw t1, 0(t1)      # get k
11            add t0, t0, t1    # add k
12            dout t0           # display sum
13            nl                # move cursor
14
15            ret               # return to caller
16 x:         .word j           # must be adjusted
17 y:         .word k           # must be adjusted
18 k:         .word 11
```

With these modifications, we now can assemble m1.a, and m2.a:

    rv m1.a
    rv m2.a

and then link the object modules—m1.o, and m2.o—produced by the assembler:

```
rv m1.o m2.o
```

and then execute the executable file created by the linker (the name of the executable file produced by the linker defaults to link.e):

```
rv link.e
```

The link.e program computes and displays the sum of i, j, and k (the sum is 23).

Overview of the Linking Process

The linker has to combine the machine code in the object modules it is linking into a single program, and then *resolve the external references*—that is, it has to adjust the addresses in the instructions that reference an external label. For example, the machine code for the jal instruction in m1.a produced by the assembler is

Address must be adjusted by linker

```
000000ef
```

Because this instruction references an external label (sub in m2.a), the assembler put all zeros in its 20-bit immediate value field. This field holds the pc-relative address to which the jal jumps. The linker has to determine the address of sub and adjust this field accordingly.

The linker also has to adjust any words created by the .word directive that specify a label operand rather than a constant. For example, consider the last three lines of m2.a:

```
x:          .word j             # must be adjusted
y:          .word k             # must be adjusted
k:          .word 11
```

The label j in the first .word directive is an external reference (j is in m1.a—the other module). Because the assembler does not know the address of j when it is assembling m2.a, it assembles the first .word directive to 0. The linker has to determine the address of j in the linked program and replace the 0 with the correct address.

The operand k in the second .word directive above is a *local reference*—that is, it is a reference to a label defined in the *same* module. The assembler assembles this .word directive to 30 hex, the address of k relative to the beginning of the m2 module. If the m1 and m2 modules are linked in that order, the m2 module is placed after the m1 module in the linked program. Thus, the address of k changes. It is now the address of k relative to the beginning of the m2 module (30 hex) *plus* the size of the m1 module (10 hex). Thus, the address of k in the linked program is 30 + 10 = 40 hex:

Before linking:
Address of k = 30

After linking:
Address of k = 10 + 30 = 40 hex

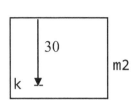

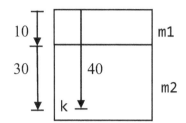

The linker must adjust the address in the location corresponding to the second `.word` directive above to reflect the new address of `k`. This location already has the address of `k` relative to the beginning of the `m2` module (from the assembler). Thus, the linker has only to add to this location the size of the `m1` module. The addresses in the two `lw` instructions in `m2.a` that reference the local labels `x` and `y` need a similar adjustment (they should be increased by 10 hex).

Linking Process in Detail

The linker cannot determine where the external or local references are from the machine code itself in the object modules produced by the assembler. For example, the machine code for the `jal` instruction in `m1.a` is

```
000000ef
```

This word, however, could be a constant rather than an instruction, in which case it would not have an address field that needs adjustment. Or it could be a `jal` instruction that references a local label, in which case its address field does not need adjustment because it holds a `pc`-relative address to a local label.

Where does the linker get the information it needs to perform the link? From the headers in the modules it is linking. Each object module consists of a header terminated by the letter C. Following the letter C is the machine code. Here are the headers in the `m1.o`, and `m2.o` object modules (obtained from the ".lst" files created by the `rv` program):

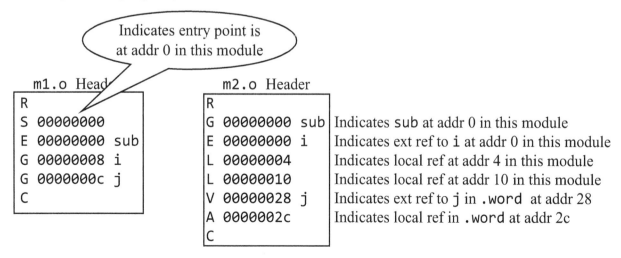

There are eight types of header entries used by the linker, each identified by the leading letter in the entry:

- R is the signature of object and executable files created by the rv program.
- An S entry provides the entry point for the program.
- A G entry provides the address and name of a global label.
- An E entry provides the address of a reference to an external label and the name of the label.
- An L entry provides the address of a *relocatable* local reference (i.e., one that needs adjustment)
- A V entry provides the address of a .word directive that references an external label, and the name of the label.
- An A entry provides the address of a .word directive that references a local label.
- C separates the header from the machine code that follows the header.

There are two more types of entries (D for a .data section and T for .text section), but they are not involved in the linking process.

The linking process consists of four steps. In the first step, the linker reads in each object module, placing the machine code for each module, one after another, into an array, which we call the *machine code array*. Thus, at the end of step 1, the machine code array contains the machine code for the entire program. In step 1, the linker also saves each header entry. The linker has a table for each type of header entry. It saves each header entry in the table for its type. For example, it saves G entries in the G table, E entries in the E table, V entries in the V table, and so on. Because each table is dedicated to only one type of header entry, there is no need to save the letter that identifies the type of the entry. For example, when it saves a G entry, it saves only the address and the label—the letter G is not saved in the G table.

When the linker saves a header entry for a module, it *adds the module's starting address to the address the entry contains*. For example, the V entry in the m2.o module for j is

        V 00000028 j

The address 00000028 is an address *relative to the beginning of the code* in m1.o. Before the linker saves this entry in the V table, it adjusts the address it contains by adding 00000010 (the address of the start of the m2 module in the machine code array) to it. Thus, the saved V entry is

        00000038 j

The adjusted address, 00000038, is an address of the external reference in the machine code array. The linker adjusts the address in every header entry in this way. Thus, at the conclusion of step 1, the addresses in the tables for the header entries are addresses *relative to the beginning of the program in the machine code array.*

When the linker reads an A entry, it enters it into the A table. But it also records in the A table the starting address in the machine code array of the module that contains the A entry. For example, when the linker is processing the A entry in m2.o,

        A 0000002c

it adjusts the address that it contains (by adding to it the address of the start of the m2 module in the machine code array). The starting address of the m2 module is 00000010. Thus, the linker adds 00000010 to 0000002c to get 0000003c. It then saves this adjusted address in the A table. But it *also* saves in the A table 00000010, the address of the start the m2 module in the machine code array. Thus, the A table entry for the A entry from the m2 module is

```
0000003c 00000010
```

Here are the header tables and the machine code array at the conclusion of step 1 (we show addresses with only 4 hex digits (16 bits) but in the tables they each occupy 32 bits):

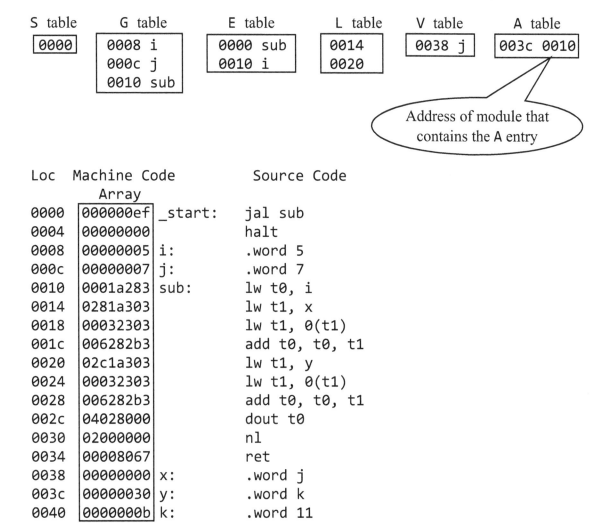

In step 2, the linker resolves external references. For each E and V table entry, the linker finds the address of the label referenced by searching the G table. It then adjusts the address field in the instruction with the external reference. For example, consider the E table entry

```
00000000 sub
```

This entry indicates that at location 0 in the machine code array there is an external reference to sub. When the linker processes this entry, it searches the G table for sub to determine the address of sub. The G entry

```
00000010 sub
```

indicates that sub is at the address 00000010. The linker then adjusts location 0 so it has the correct address of sub in the correct format.

In step 3, the linker processes the A table entries. For each A table entry, it adds the module address for that entry (obtained from table entry) to the location in the machine code array specified by the entry. For example, for the A entry

```
0000003c 00000010
```

it adds the address (00000010) of the module that contains the A entry to the location in the machine code array at the address 0000003c, transforming it from 00000030 to 00000040, which is the address of k in the machine code array.

In step 4, the final step of the linking process, the linker outputs the executable file. It outputs the header for the executable file, the letter C, and the machine code in that order. The header consists of all the entries in the S, G, and A tables. The V entries are outputted as A entries because they now correspond to local addresses. All the external references are now resolved so the E and V entries are not outputted. The L entries also are not outputted. L entries point to instructions that have gp-relative addresses. After link time, these gp-relative addresses never change. Thus, the L entries are not needed.

Here is a display of the header and the machine code for the executable file produced by the linker after linking m1.o, and m2.o (compare with the contents of the machine code array before modification by the linker shown above):

```
Header
R
S 00000000
G 00000008 i
G 0000000c j
G 00000010 sub
A 00000038
A 0000003c
C


Loc      Code
0000   010000ef <- adjusted (was 000000ef from jal sub)
0004   00000000
0008   00000005
000c   00000007
0010   0081a283 <- adjusted (was 0001a283 from lw t0, i)
0014   0381a303 <- adjusted (was 0281a303 from lw t1, x)
0018   00032303
001c   006282b3
0020   03c1a303 <- adjusted (was 02c1a303 from lw t1, y)
0024   00032303
0028   006282b3
002c   04028000
0030   02000000
0034   00008067
0038   0000000c
003c   00000040 <- adjusted (was 00000030 from .word k)
0040   0000000b
```

Startup Code

C programs are always linked with a module called *startup code*. When a compiled C program is invoked, the operating system loads it into memory and then transfers control to startup code—not to the `main` function. Startup code performs some initializations necessary to support the command line arguments and the C library functions. It then calls the `main` function in the C program. When the `main` function completes, it returns to its caller (which is startup code). Startup code does some final housekeeping and then returns to `rv`.

Before startup code calls `main`, it constructs the `argc` and `argv` arguments that startup code passes to the `main` function. These arguments provide to `main` the command line arguments specified on the command line when the executable program is invoked. For example, suppose on a Linux system the C program in the file `t.c` is compiled, producing the executable file `t`. If this program is then invoked with

```
t p1 p2
```

the operating system makes this raw command line available to startup code. From this command line, startup code constructs the `argc` and `argv` arguments and then calls `main`, passing it `argc` and `argv`. For the command line above, startup code produces `argc` and `argv` configured as follows:

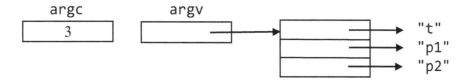

`argc` is the count of the number of command line arguments (including the name of the program that is invoked). `argv` is a pointer to first slot of an array of character pointers. The successive slots of this array point to the successive command line arguments. Each slot of this array is a `char` pointer. Thus, `argv` is a pointer to a `char` pointer. Accordingly, in `main`, the `argv` argument should be declared in the C program as a pointer to a `char` pointer:

```
int main(int argc, char **argv)
```

Read "`char **argv`" as "`argv` is a pointer to a `char` pointer". This declaration consists of two parts: "`*argv`" (read as "`argv` is a pointer") and "`char *`" (read as "to a `char` pointer"). An equivalent way of declaring `argv` which is less confusing to some is

```
int main(int argc, char *argv[])
```

The empty square brackets following a parameter indicates that the parameter is a pointer. Thus, `argv[]` is equivalent to `*argv`, which in turn means `char *argv[]` is equivalent to `char **argv`. Both versions declare `argv` as a pointer to a `char` pointer.

Let's review what happens when a C compiler compiles a C program. The typical C compiler consists of four parts: the preprocessor, the translator, the assembler, and the linker. The preprocessor reads in the source program and handles all the preprocessor statements in the source code (i.e., the statements that start with the pound sign). For example, for an `#include` statement, the preprocessor reads in the specified file and inserts it into the source code. The output of the preprocessor is the source program as modified by the preprocessor. The next part—the translator—of the compiler translates the modified source code to assembly language. The third part assembles the assembly code produced by the translator. The final part—the linker—links the object module produced by the assembler part with the startup code module and any other modules the program needs. For example, if the C program calls `printf`, then the `printf` object module—obtained from the C library—is linked with the compiled program along with the startup code. The following diagram illustrates this process:

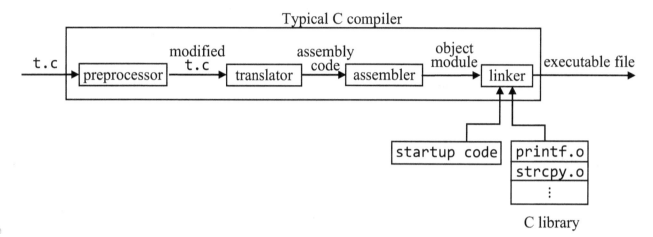

For example, here is a C program (it is in the file `t.c`) that displays the arguments given on the command line when it is invoked:

t.c

```
 1 #include <stdio.h>
 2 int main(int argc, char *argv[])
 3 {
 4     while (1)                       // 1 represents true
 5     {
 6         argc--;                     // decrement index into argv
 7         if (argc < 0) break;        // exit loop when argc goes neg
 8         printf("%s\n", argv[argc]); // display command line argument
 9     }
10     return 0;                       // return to startup code
11 }
```

On each iteration of the loop, the command line argument that `argv[argc]` points to is displayed by the `printf` statement. `argc`, which initially equals the number of command line arguments, is decremented on each iteration. Thus, a different command line argument is displayed on each iteration. To preprocess, translate to assembly language, assemble, and link this program with the **gcc** C compiler, enter

        gcc t.c -o t

gcc then outputs the executable file `t.exe` (or `t` on non-Windows systems). If we then run the program by entering

        t p1 p2

the program displays the command line arguments in last-to-first order. We see on the screen

```
p2
p1
t
```

We can mimic this process with our rv program. But unfortunately, we do not have a C compiler that outputs RISC-V assembly code. So we have to compile our C program to assembly language ourselves. We do this to get the file t.a. We then assemble t.a to get the object file t.o:

```
rv t.a       (creates object file t.o)
```

The file su.o in the software package for this textbook is the object code for startup code. It creates the argc and argv arguments and passes them to the translated main function in our C program. To create an executable file from t.o and su.o, we link them:

```
rv su.o t.o -o t.e
```

Name of output file

to get the executable file t.e. The -o command line argument is used to specify the output file name (without the -o switch, the output file name defaults to link.e). Finally, we execute t.e with

```
rv t.e p1 p2
```

The rv program, which acts like the operating system, loads the program in t.e into memory and passes the command line to startup code in t.e. The startup code then constructs the argc and argv arguments and calls main, passing it the argc and argv arguments in a0 and a1. When the main function in t.e completes, it returns to the startup code. Startup code then returns to the rv program. We see on the display the command line arguments in last-to-first order:

```
p2
p1
t.e
```

Here is the assembler code for our startup code:

```
                              su.a
 1│# Start-up code that configures argc and argv and calls main
 2│          .extern main      # needed to link to main
 3│_start:   li t3, 0xc000     # t3 points to command line
 4│          la t4, array      # t4 point to array
 5│          li a0, 0          # a0 is argc counter
 6│          li t1, ' '        # used to determine if at end of arg
 7│
 8│getarg:   sw t3, 0(t4)      # store arg addr in array   ←─────┐
 9│          addi t4, t4, 4    # inc pointer to array            │
10│          addi a0, a0, 1    # increment argc counter          │
11│                                                              │
12│nextchar: addi t3, t3, 1       # move com line pointer ←───┐  │
13│          lbu t0, 0(t3)        # get char from com line    │  │
14│          beq t0, x0, callmain # is it the null char       │  │
15│          bne t0, t1, nextchar # compare char and blank ───┘  │
16│                                                              │
17│          sb x0, 0(t3)      # overlay blank with null char    │
18│          addi t3, t3, 1    # advance ptr to next arg         │
19│          jal x0, getarg ──────────────────────────────────┘
20│
21│callmain: lw a1, argv       # call main passing argc (a0), argv (a1)
22│          jal ra, main      # program must have main function
23│
24│alldone:  halt
25│argv:     .word array       # address of argv array
26│array:    .zero 100         # 25-word argv array
```

The rv program provides the command line to the startup code by placing the command line at location
c000 hex in the form of a single null-terminated string, with a single space between command line
arguments. Suppose we invoke the program in t.e with

      rv t.e p1 p2

Then on entry into the startup code, these are the structures that exist:

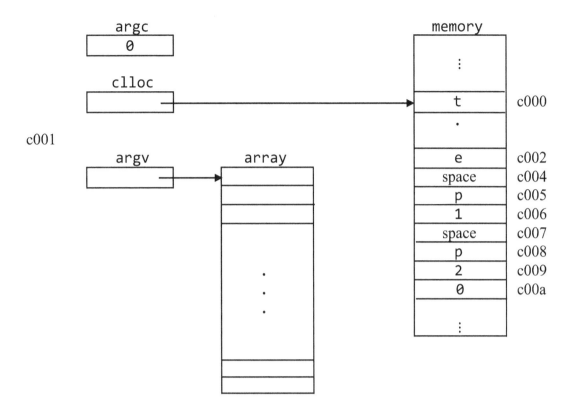

The loop that starts at line 8 in `su.a` scans the command line in memory looking for the space character (20 hex) at the end of each command line argument (except for the last one, which is terminated with the null character). It replaces each space character with the null character (see line 17). Thus, when startup code finishes scanning the command line, each command line argument is a separate null-terminated string. During this scan, startup code also places the address of the start of each command line argument into the next available slot in `array` (see line 8). It also increments the `argc` counter in `a0` for each command line argument (see line10). This procedure transforms the initial structure shown above to the structure below. Line 22 calls `main`.

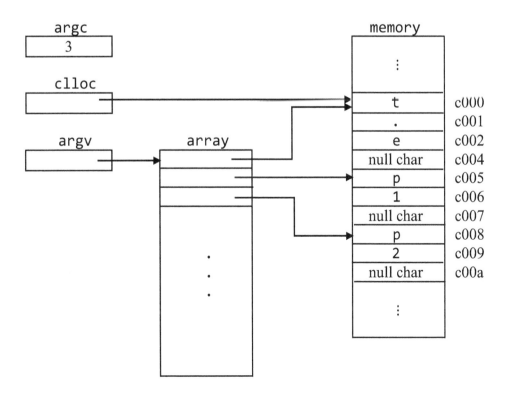

Because line 22 in startup code calls main, every C program must have a main function. If we change the label in lines 2 and 22 from main to rabbit, then every C program would have to have a rabbit function instead of a main function. Most compilers provide the source code for the startup module. Thus, if you are tired of the name "main", you can replace it in the source code for the startup module, re-assemble the startup module, and then use your chosen name in place of "main" in your C programs.

Here is the assembly language program in t.a that corresponds to the C program in t.c (the C code appears as comments in t.a):

```
                                    t.a
 1  |                                # #include <stdio.h>
 2  |          .global main          # int main(int argc, char *argv[])
 3  | main:                          # {
 4  |                                #     while (1
 5  |                                #     {
 6  | @L0:     addi a0, a0, -1       #         argc--;
 7  |
 8  |          blt a0, x0, @L1       #         if (argc < 0) break;
 9  |
10  |          mv t0, a0             #         printf("%s\n", argv[argc]);
11  |          slli t0, t0, 2
12  |          add t0, t0, a1
13  |          lw t0, 0(t0)
14  |          sout t0
15  |          nl
16  |
17  |          j @L0                 #     }
18  |
19  | @L1:     li a0, 0              #     return 0;
20  |          ret
21  |                                # }
```

1 is always true but no infinite loop because of break

Dereferences pointer in t0

A real C compile would translate the printf statement in the C program to a call of the printf function in the C library. However, we simply translate it to inline code. The while loop displays the command line arguments in last-to-first order. Each time through the loop, the sout instruction (line 14) displays the command line argument that argv[argc] points to. Each time through the loop, argc is decremented. Thus, a different command line argument is displayed on each iteration of the loop.

argc is in a0, and argv is in a1. a1 contains the address of array (see arrow *a* in the diagram that follows). Line 10 loads t0 with a copy of argc. Line 11 multiplies it by 4 (by shifting the contents of t0 two positions to the left). Why multiply by 4? Because each slot of array is 4 bytes. Line 12 adds the address of array (in a1) to t0. At this point t0 points to the slot in array that in turn points to a command line argument (see arrow *b*). Next, line 13 dereferences the pointer in t0, after which t0 points to the command line argument to be displayed (see arrow *c*). Finally, line 14 displays this command line argument. The j pseudoinstruction on line 17 jumps back to the beginning of the loop.

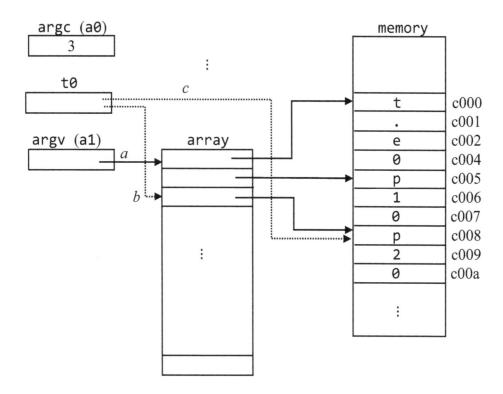

Problems

1) Disassemble the following hex display of an object module. That is, convert it back to the assembly language program from which it was assembled.

```
 0:   524C 0000 0000 4C04 0000 0045 1000 0000     RL....L....E....
10:   7A00 4718 0000 0078 0047 1C00 0000 7900     z.G....x.G....y.
20:   411C 0000 0043 83A2 8101 03A3 C101 0323     A....C.........#
30:   0300 B382 6200 23A0 6100 0000 0000 0500     ....b.#.a.......
40:   0000 1800 0000                              ......
```

2) Using the same format used in the ".lst" files produced by the rv program, show the contents of the object file assembled from the following module :

```
        .start s
        .extern a
        .extern b
        .global c
        lw t0, a
        lw t1, b
        add t0, t0, t1
        sw t0, c
s:      halt
c:      .word 0
x:      .word c
```

3) Using the same format used in the ".1st" files produced by the rv program, show the contents of the object file assembled from the following module:

```
        .extern sub
        jal sub
        la r0, sub+4
        lw t1, x
        jal ra, 0(t1)
        halt
x:      .word sub
```

4) Can the header in an object module have multiple E entries for the same label? If so, show an assembly language program that will produce such a header. Can the header have multiple G entries for the same label? If so, show an assembly language program that will produce such a header.

5) Where are .global, .extern, and .start directives allowed in a program. Determine your answer by running test programs with rv.

6) What are the advantages of having a linking capability?

7) The adjustment required by a jal instruction that make an external reference is different from the adjustment required by a lw instruction because they have different formats. How does the linker know which adjustment to perform? Both external references are represented by an E entry in the header.

8) Why is an external reference made by a .word directive represented by a V entry in the header but an external reference made by a jal or lw instruction is represented by an E entry?

9) The startup code in su.a terminates with a halt instruction. How would startup code for a Linux computer system terminate?

10) The size of array in startup code is 25 words. Does this set the limit on the number of command line arguments to 25?

11) Try linking a module that has a .data directive. What happens? Why would upgrading the linker so that it could handle .data directives require a major upgrade of the linker?

12) Suppose p1.a and p2.a are the following assembly language modules:

```
        p1.a                          p2.a
        .global x                     .global a
        .extern a           a:        .word 1000
x:      .word 5
y:      .word a
```

Using the same format used in the ".1st" files produced by the rv program, show the contents of the object files produced when p1.a and p2.a are assembled. Show the contents of the executable file produced when p2.o and p1.o are linked in that order.

13) What is displayed when q1.a and q2.a are assembled, linked in q1-q2 order, and run? When linked in q2-q1 order and run? Assume memory is zeroed out before the executable program is loaded.

```
            q1.a                              q2.a
        .extern y                         .global y
        lw t0, x+4          x:            .word 0x04010000
        hout t0            y:             .word 0x08010000
        lw t0, y-4                        .word 0
        hout t0
        halt
x:      .word 5
```

14) Can a label appear in one module without a .global for it and appear in another module in the same program with a .global directive. Justify your answer.

15) The following program has an error. When is it detected? At compile time, assembly time, link time, or run time? Justify your answer.

```
#include <stdio.h>
int main()
{
    printff("hello\n");
    return 0;
}
```

16) Is there any advantage in linking startup code first? Is there any disadvantage? Justify your answers.

17) Write, assemble, link with startup code, and run a program that consists of three modules: z1.a, z2.a, and z3.a. z1.a reads in a positive integer n and passes it to z2.a. z2.a then displays all the squares from 1 to n. z2.a determines each square by calling z3.a, passing it the number to be squared. z3.a returns the square. To determine the square of i, sum the first i positive odd integers. For example, the square of 3 is the sum of the first 3 positive odd integers: $1+3+5 = 9 = 3^2$.

18) Write an assembly language program this is passed two single-digit ASCII strings from the command line. Your program should display the sum of the two digits it is passed. Assemble, link with su.o, and run using the rv program. Test your program with 5 and 7. *Hint*: Convert the command line arguments from their ASCII codes to the numbers they represent.

19) Translate the following program to assembly language. Assemble, link with su.o, and run using the rv program:

```
// rx0619.c Run with args "first second third"
#include <stdio.h>
int main(int argc, char *argv[])
{
    printf("%s\n", argv[argc - 1]);
    printf("%s\n", argv[0]);
    printf("%d\n", argc);
    return 0;
}
```

20) Translate the following program to assembly language. Assemble, link with su.o, and run using the rv program:

```
// rx0620.c Run with args "first second third"
#include <stdio.h>
int main(int argc, char *argv[])
{
    while (--argc)
        printf("%d %s\n", argc, argv[argc]);
    return 0;
}
```

7 Compiling C Code to RISC-V

Quick Introduction to C

Because we are about to examine how C code is compiled to RISC-V assembly language, let's take a quick look at the C programming language. A C program consists of one or more *functions*, one of which must be `main` (because startup code calls `main`). One function can call another. The calling function is referred to as the *caller*; the called function is referred to as the *callee*. A called function can in turn call a function. For example, suppose `main` calls a function `f`, and `f` calls a function g. Then `main` is a caller. g is a callee. `f` is both a callee with respect to function `main`, and a caller with respect to g.

A C compiler typically translates the C code in its input file to assembly language, and then translates the assembly language version of the program to machine language. The following diagram illustrates this process:

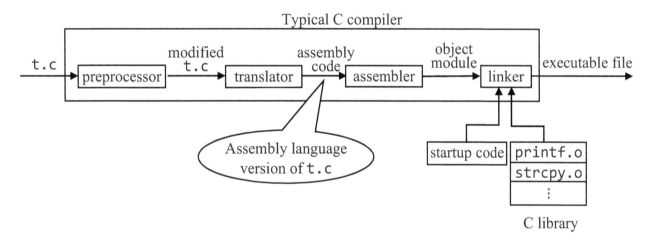

Most compilers will output not only the executable file for the program but also its assembly language version if the appropriate command line argument (`-S` for most compilers) is specified on the command line. For example, if the `gcc` C compiler on Linux is invoked with

```
gcc t.c -S -o t
```

it outputs an executable file named `t` and a text file named `t.s` that contains the assembly language version of the C code in the input file `t.c`.

There are four types of variables in C:

- global variables
- static local variables
- dynamic local variables
- parameters

A *global variable* is a variable that is declared *outside* a function. Its *scope* (i.e., where it can be used in the program) extends from its declaration to the end of the file, excluding those regions of a program that are within the scope of an identically-named local variable or parameter. Its scope also extends to separately-compiled functions that are part of the same program. In the assembly language version of the program produced by the compiler, a global variable appears as a .word directive (for single-word global variables) or as a .zero or .space directive (for multiple-word global variables). For example, if a global variable x is declared with

```
int x = 1;
```

then in the assembly language version of the program there will appear the following .word directive:

```
x:          .word 1
```

This .word directive reserves and initializes a word in the executable file:

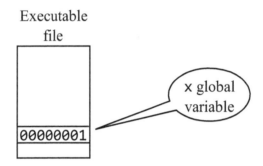

Thus, even before the program is loaded into memory, the global variable exists and has been initialized. For this reason, we say that global variables are created and initialized *at assembly time* when the assembler translates their .word directives.

A *static local variable* is a variable that is declared *inside* a function whose declaration includes the **static** keyword. The scope of a static local variable is the function in which it is declared. Like global variables, static local variables are created by .word, .zero, or .space directives in the assembly language version of the program. Thus, like global variables, static local variables are created and initialized at assembly time.

A *dynamic local variable* is a variable that is declared *inside* a function whose declaration does *not* include the keyword **static**. Its scope is the function in which it is declared. Dynamic local variables are *dynamic*. That is, they are created and destroyed during the execution of a program. The dynamic local variables in a function are created every time that function is called, and destroyed when the function returns to its caller.

A *parameter* is a variable that receives the value of an argument in a function call. Its scope is the function in which it is a parameter. Parameters for a function are created when the function is called and are destroyed when the function returns to its caller.

The following C program illustrates the four types of variables:

r0701.c

```
 1 #include <stdio.h>          // stdio.h has prototype for printf
 2 void f(int z);              // function prototype
 3 int x = 1;                  // global variable
 4 int main(void)             // int is the return type
 5 {
 6     f(x);                  // pass f the value of x
 7     f(x+10);               // pass f the value of x+10
 8     return 0;              // return 0 to the operating system
 9 }
10 #================================================================
11 void f(int z)              // z is the parameter
12 {
13     int a = 2;             // dynamic local variable
14     static int b = 3;      // static local variable
15     printf("%d\n", z);     // displays 1 (1st call)  12 (2nd call)
16     printf("%d\n", a);     // displays 2 (1st call)   2 (2nd call)
17     printf("%d\n", b);     // displays 3 (1st call)   4 (2nd call)
18     printf("%d\n", x);     // displays 1 (1st call)   2 (2nd call)
19     a++;                   // increment a
20     b++;                   // increment b
21     x++;                   // increment x
22 }
```

The call of the each `printf` statement (lines 15 through 18) displays in decimal the value of the second argument in each call. The "%d" in the first argument specifies that the values should be displayed in decimal. The "\n" in the first argument specifies that the cursor should move to the next line after the value is displayed. Thus, lines 15 through 18 display the values of z, a, b, and x on successive lines of the display.

Each time `f` is called, the dynamic local variable a is created and initialized to 2 (by code at the beginning of f). It is destroyed on exit. Thus, although on exit its value is 3, that value is lost. On the second call it is again created and initialized to 2. Thus, on both calls, line 16 displays 2. The scope of a is the function `f`. Thus, it cannot be accessed from outside f—for example, from `main`.

Like the dynamic local variable a, the scope of b is the function `f`. Thus, it cannot be accessed from outside `f`. However, unlike the dynamic local variable a, the static local variable b is *not* created and initialized by code at the beginning the `f`. It is created and initialized by a `.word` directive whose operand is 3 in the corresponding assembly language program. On the first call of f, the value of b is its initial value 3 which is displayed by line 17. b is then incremented to 4 on line 20. Thus, on the second call of `f`, the value of b is is 4, which is displayed by line 17. Note that it retains its value from one call to the next. On exit from the first call of `f`, b is 4. Thus, on entry into `f` on the second call, b is 4—not 3. It is not reinitialized to 3 on each call as line 14 seems to suggest.

The variable x is a global variable. Thus, it can be accessed both from within `main` and from within `f`. Like the static local variable b, it is created by a `.word` directive that initializes it to 1. On the first call of `f`, x is 1. It is incremented to 2 on line 21. Thus, on entry into `f` on the second call, x is 2.

Line 2 in `r0701.c` is an example of a prototype. A *prototype* of a function is essentially the first line of a function's definition terminated by a semicolon. When the compiler is scanning the calls of `f` on lines 6 and 7, it checks the arguments in the calls to see if they are compatible with the parameters in the function definition. But to do this, it needs to have already scanned the function's definition or the function's prototype. That is, either the function definition or its prototype must *precede* the function calls. Because the function definition *follows* the calls in this program, a prototype is needed that precedes the function calls. If, however, the order of `main` and `f` were reversed, then the definition of `f` would precede the calls. In that case, the prototype would be unnecessary. The prototype for the `printf` library function is in the header file `stdio.h`. That is why we have to include `stdio.h` (see line 1).

`main` returns the return code 0 to startup code on line 8 (a 0 return code indicates a normal termination). Startup code then returns this 0 return code to the operating system. Because `main` returns an integer, its definition starts with "`int`", which indicates that it returns a value whose type is `int`. If a function does not return anything to its caller, the return type specified at the start of its definition should be "`void`" (see line 11).

The C programming language supports pointer variables. For example, the following declaration declares p to be an integer pointer (read "*" as "pointer"):

```
int *p;    // declare p an int pointer
```

Suppose x is declared with

```
int x;    // declare x as an int
```

Then the statement

```
p = &x;    // assign p the address of x
```

assigns the address of x to p ("&" is the *address-of operator*). Because p then contains the address of x, we say that "p points to x." To access what is in p, we write "p" in a C program . But to access what p points to, we write "*p". For example, the following statement assigns 5 not to p but to the location p points to:

```
*p = 5;
```

When we use the address in p to access the word at that address, we say we are *dereferencing* p.

In `r0702.c`, `main` passes the address of x to the parameter p in `add1`. `add1` dereferences p to get the value in x. It adds 1 to this value. It then dereferences p a second time to put the new value back into the location p points to (which is x) Thus, the before-call value of x is 7; its after-call value is 8.

y and its corresponding parameter a are distinct variables. They occupy different locations in memory. Thus, when f increments a, it has no effect on y. Thus, y is 11 both before and after the call of f.

z is a global variable whose initial value is 13. It is incremented by 1 on line 7. Thus, its before-call value is 13; its after-call value is 14.

r0702.c

```
 1 #include <stdio.h>
 2 int z = 13;
 3 void add1(int *p, int a)
 4 {
 5     *p = *p + 1;    // increments value in x
 6     a = a + 1;      // increments parameter a, no effect on y
 7     z = z + 1;      //  increments global variable z
 8 }
 9 #===============================================================
10 int main(void)
11 {
12     int x = 7, y = 11;
13     printf("%d %d %d\n", x, y, z);  // displays 7 11 13
14     add1(&x, y);
15     printf("%d %d %d\n", x, y, z);  // displays 8 11 14
16     return 0;
17 }
```

Using Registers to Hold Variables

If a dynamic local variable needs to be preserved across a function call it is mapped to a callee-saved register (registers s0 through s11). However, if the C code requires the memory address of the variable, then such a variable is not mapped to a register (because then it would not have a memory address). Instead it is allocated on the stack so it has an address. For example, if a C function starts this way,

```
void f(void)
{
    int x = 5, *p;    // x on the stack, p in s0
    p = &x;           // assign p the address of x
        ⋮
}
```

then x is allocated on the stack because the assignment statement needs the address of x. Thus, the corresponding assembler code (assuming f does not call a function) is

```
f:      addi sp, sp, -4  # allocate space on stack for x
        li t0, 5
        sw t0, 0(sp)      # initialize x with 5
        mov s0, sp        # Assign address of x (in sp) to p (s0)
            ⋮
        addi sp, sp, 4    # deallocate x
        jalr x0, 0(ra)    # return to caller
```

Global variables and static local variables are created and initialized at assembly time with `.word`, `.zero`, or `.space` directives. Thus, they are not mapped to registers.

The registers `a0` through `a7` are for passing arguments. They also serve as the corresponding parameters. However, if the C code requires the address of a parameter, then its value must be pushed onto the stack so that it has a memory address.

The big advantage of using registers is that it can substantially reduce execution time. Accessing data in a register requires less time than accessing data in memory. Moreover, register access does not require the load-store overload associated with variables in memory. For example, suppose we want to add 5 to the variable x which is in the `s0` register. We need only one instruction:

```
addi s0, s0, 5
```

But to add 5 to x in memory, we need three instructions:

```
lw t0, x
addi t0, t0, 5
sw t0, x
```

Let's now examine the assembly code in `r0701.a`—the assembly code corresponding to the C program in `r0701.c`. The assembly code is commented with its corresponding C code:

r0701.a

```
 1                                # #include <stdio.h>
 2                                # void f(int z);
 3  x:         .word 1            # int x = 1;
 4  main:      .global main       # int main()
 5             addi sp, sp -4     # {
 6             sw ra, 0(sp)
 7
 8             lw a0, x           #    f(x);
 9             jal ra, f
10
11             lw a0, x           #    f(x+10);
12             addi a0, a0, 10
13             jal ra, f
14
15             lw ra, 0(sp)       #    return 0;
16             addi sp, sp, 4
17             li a0, 0
18             jalr x0, 0(ra)     # }
19  #========================================================
20  f:         .global f          # void f(int z)
21             addi sp, sp, -4    # {
22             sw s0, 0(sp)
23
24             li s0, 2           #    int a = 2;
25                                #    static int b = 3;
26             dout a0            #    printf("%d\n", z);
27             nl
28
29             dout s0            #    printf("%d\n", a);
30             nl
31
32             lw t0, @1b         #    printf("%d\n", b);
33             dout t0
34             nl
35
36             lw t0, x           #    printf("%d\n", x);
37             dout t0
38             nl
39
40             addi s0, s0, 1     #    a++;
41
42             lw  t0, @1b        #    b++;
43             addi t0, t0, 1
44             sw t0, @1b
45
46             lw t0, x           #    x++;
47             addi t0, t0, 1
48             sw t0, x
49
50             lw s0, 0(sp)       # }
51             addi sp, sp, 4
52             jalr x0, 0(ra)
53
54  @1b:       .word 3
```

No initialization code for b

The global variable x is created with a .word directive on line 3:

```
3 x:            .word 1                 # int x = 1;
```

Function names in C are global, whether or not they are called from a separately-compiler module. Thus, main and f are declared global on lines 4 and 20, respectively:

```
 4 main:       .global main            # int main()
               ...
20 f:          .global f               # void f(int z)
```

To pass x to f, the calling sequence for the first call loads the global variable x from memory into a0 (recall the registers a0 through a7 are for passing arguments in function calls):

```
8              lw a0, x                 #    f(x);
9              jal ra, f
```

The calling sequence for the second call computes the value of the argument (x + 10) before executing the jal instruction:

```
11             lw a0, x                 #    f(x+10);
12             addi a0, a0, 10
13             jal ra, f
```

The jal instruction on line 9 in main that calls f loads ra with the return address for that call, overlaying the return address main needs to return to its caller. Thus, main has to save ra on line 6 so it can restore it with the return address it needs to return to its caller (startup code). It reserves space on the stack for ra by decrementing sp by 4 on line 5:

```
5              addi sp, sp -4
6              sw ra, 0(sp)
```

Before main returns to its caller, line 15 restores ra with the value it had on entry into main:

```
15             lw ra, 0(sp)
```

Line 16 adds 4 to sp, restoring it with its original value. Line 17 initializes a0 with the return code, Then the jalr instruction on line 18 returns to startup code with a return code of 0 in a0 (recall a0 and a1 are the registers for returning values to the caller):

```
16             addi sp, sp, 4
17             li a0, 0
18             jalr x0, 0(ra)
```

In f, s0 is used for the dynamic local variable a. Line 24 initializes a to 2:

```
24             li s0, 2                 #    int a = 2;
```

Because s0 is callee-saved register, f saves it on the stack (line 22) and then restores it (line 50) before returning to its caller:

```
22              sw s0, 0(sp)
                ...
50              lw s0, 0(sp)                # }
```

The compiler should have used a caller-saved register instead of the callee-saved register s0 for the variable a—then the save and restore would be unnecessary.

sp is also a callee-saved register. Thus, f is obligated to return to its caller with the same value in sp that was in sp on entry into f. It does this by incrementing sp by 4 on line 51:

```
51              addi sp, sp, 4
```

f decrements sp on line 5. Thus, incrementing sp by 4 on line 51 returns sp to its original value. Similarly, main is obligated to return to its caller (startup code) with the same value in sp that was in sp on entry into main. It does this by incrementing sp by 4 on line 16.

Note that there is *no* code corresponding to the declaration and initialization of the static local variable b on line 25:

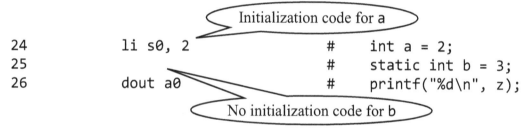

```
24              li s0, 2              #     int a = 2;
25                                    #     static int b = 3;
26              dout a0               #     printf("%d\n", z);
```

b is created and initialized by the .word directive on line 54:

```
54 @1b:        .word 3
```

Thus, it is not reinitialized each time f is called. In contrast, there *is* code corresponding to the declaration and initialization of the dynamic local variable a on line 24. The register s0 is used for a. Thus, each time f is called, s0 is allocated for a and is reinitialized to 2. Thus, in a sense, the a variable is "created" on each call of f. When f returns to its caller, s0 reverts back to the caller's value. Thus, in a sense, the variable a in "destroyed" when f returns to its caller.

The name of the global variable x in the C program is also its name in the corresponding assembly language program. However, the static local variable b has a different name—@1b—in the assembly language program. Its C-level name is prefixed with "@" and a sequence number. If there were more static local variables in the C program, the names would be prefixed with "@2", "@3", and so on, in the assembly language program. To see why this prefixing is necessary, consider a program with the following structure:

```
void f(void)
{
    static int a;
    ...
}
int main(void)
{
    static int a;
    f();
    return 0;
}
```

In both functions, the name of the static local variable is a. This is perfectly legal because they both have local scope. Thus, there is never any ambiguity on which a is being referenced. A reference to a in f is a reference to its a; a reference to a in main is a reference to its a. Because the two static local variables are distinct variables, each is represented in the corresponding assembly language program with its own .word directive. The scope of a label in an assembly language file is the *entire file* (with a .global directive, it scope also extends to other files). Thus, in our example, if the label a is used on both .word directives, any reference to a would be ambiguous. The assembler would flag this problem with a "Duplicate label" error message. However, the compiler avoids this problem by adding a unique prefix to the names of static local variables at the assembly level. For this example, the name of a in f would be @1a at the assembly level; the name of the variable a in main would be @2a—distinct names so no conflict.

The compiler prefixes all the labels it generates with "@"—not just the labels on static local variables. C identifiers cannot start with "@". Thus, there is never any conflict between compiler-generated names and C-level names that are used unchanged at the assembly level.

To run the program in r0701.a, first assemble it by entering

        rv r0701.a

Then link the object file r0701.o the assembler produces with startup code by entering

        rv su.o r0701.o

Then execute the executable file link.e that the linker produces by entering

        rv link.e

Now let's turn our attention to r0702.a, the assembly language program that corresponds to the C program in r0702.c:

```
                              r0702.a
 1                              # #include <stdio.h>
 2 z:        .word 13           # int z = 13;
 3 add1:     .global add1       # void add1(int *p, int a)
 4                              # {
 5           lw t0, 0(a0)       #     *p = *p + 1;
 6           addi t0, t0, 1
 7           sw t0, 0(a0)
 8
 9           addi a1, a1, 1     #     a = a + 1;
10
11           lw t0, z           #     z = z + 1;
12           addi t0, t0, 1
13           sw t0, z
14
15           jalr x0, 0(ra)     # }
16 # ==============================================================
17 main:     .global main       # int main()
18           addi sp, sp, -12   # {
19           sw ra, 8(sp)
20           sw s0, 4(sp)
21
22           li t0, 7           #     int x = 7, y = 11;
23           sw t0, 0(sp)
24           li s0, 11
25
26           lw t0, 0(sp)       #     printf("%d %d %d\n", x, y, z);
27           dout t0
28           li t0, ' '
29           aout t0
30           dout s0
31           aout t0
32           lw t0, z
33           dout t0
34           nl
35
36           mv a0, sp          #     add1(&x, y);
37           mv a1, s0
38           jal ra, add1
39
40           lw t0, 0(sp)       #     printf("%d %d %d\n", x, y, z);
41           dout t0
42           li t0, ' '
43           aout t0
44           dout s0
45           aout t0
46           lw t0, z
47           dout t0
48           nl
49
50           li a0, 0           #     return 0;
51           lw s0, 4(sp)
52           lw ra, 8(sp)
53           addi sp, sp, 12
54           jalr x0, 0(ra)     # }
```

In `r0702.a`, the dynamic local variable x is created and initialized on the stack because its address is needed in the call of add1:

```
36              mv a0, sp            #    add1(&x, y);
37              mv a1, s0
38              jal ra, add1
```

The first argument is the address of x (recall "&" is the address-of operator in C). For x to have an address, it must be in memory. On entry, main reserves space on the stack for x as well as for ra and s0, by decrementing sp by 12 (we need three words on the stack which is 12 bytes):

```
18              addi sp, sp, -12
```

ra and s0 are saved on the stack because main uses them, and they are callee-saved registers:

```
19              sw ra, 8(sp)
20              sw s0, 4(sp)
```

After the decrementation of sp by 12, sp has the address of x (sp + 4 is the address of the word for s0, and sp + 8 is the address of the word for ra):

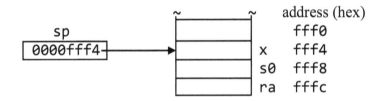

Thus, to initialize the stack word corresponding to x to 7, on line 23 we store 7 in the location sp points to:

```
22              li t0, 7             #    int x = 7;
23              sw t0, 0(sp)
```

Before returning to its caller, main has to restore s0, ra, and sp with their values on entry. main restores s0 and ra by loading with their original values that were previously saved on the stack:

```
51              lw s0, 4(sp)
52              lw ra, 8(sp)
```

main then restores sp by incrementing it by 12, which also in effect pops x and the values saved for s0 and ra:

```
53              addi sp, sp, 12
```

On entry into `add1`, `a0` holds the parameter `p`, which is the address of `x`. To access what `p` is pointing to (which is `x`), `a0` is dereferenced twice: once on line 5 to load `t0` from `x`, and one on line 7 to store a new value into `x`:

```
5               lw t0, 0(a0)        #    *p = *p + 1;
6               addi t0, t0, 1
7               sw t0, 0(a0)
```

The effect is to increase the value in `x` by 1. Line 9 increments the parameter `a` (which is in `a1`):

```
9               addi a1, a1, 1      #    a = a + 1;
```

The argument `y` in the call of `add1` on line 36 corresponds to the parameter `a` in the `add1` function. Because `y` and `a` are in different locations (`y` is in `s0`, `a` is in `a0`), line 9 (which increments `a`) has no effect on `y`:

```
9               addi a1, a1, 1      #    a = a + 1;
```

Thus, before and after the call of `add1`, `y` is 11. The global variable `z` is incremented in `add1` on lines 11, 12, and 13:

```
11              lw t0, z            #    z = z + 1;
12              addi t0, t0, 1
13              sw t0, z
```

Thus, its value, like the value of `x` is changed by the call of `add1`.

To run the program in `r0702.a`, enter

```
rv r0702.a              (to assemble)
rv su.o r0702.o         (to link with startup code)
rv link.e               (to execute the linked program)
```

It will then display

```
7 11 13
8 11 14
```

Compiling Control Structures

Compiling the control structures in C, such as `if`, `while` and `do-while`, to RISC-V is a straight-forward process. Simply test the condition specified in the control structure with a branch or set-compare instruction. Then branch or not according to the result of the test. It general, how to translate a control structure is obvious. However, the obvious translation of the `while` statement is not the best translation. Consider the following `while` statement:

```
while (x)
{
    printf("%x", x);
    x--;
}
```

In C, any nonzero value represents true; zero represents false. Thus, if x is initially 5 when the while statement above is executed, its body will be executed five times (for x = 5, 4, 3, 2, and 1). When x reaches 0, the exit from the loop occurs. Let's translates this statement to assembly code in the obvious way. Assume s0 holds x. Here is the code we get:

```
@L0:        beq s0, x0, @L1        # while (x)
                                   # {
            dout s0                #     printf("%d", x)
            addi s0, s0, -1        #     x--;
            jal x0, @L0            # }
@L1:
```

On each iteration of the loop, two transfer-of-control instructions (beq and jal) are executed. But consider this alternate translation:

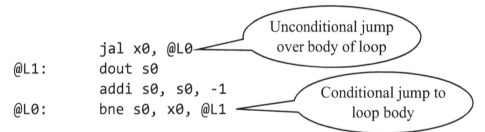

```
            jal x0, @L0
@L1:        dout s0
            addi s0, s0, -1
@L0:        bne s0, x0, @L1
```

In this version, the jal instruction branches over the body of the loop to the exit test code, which now follows the body of the loop. In this version, the jal instruction is executed only once. In the obvious version, it is executed on each iteration. Both versions require four words, but the alternate version executes fewer instructions if the loop reiterates at least two times.

Compiling Structs and Arrays

Global and static local C structs and arrays are created with .word, .zero, or .space directives. Dynamic local structs and arrays are created on the stack. For example, consider the following assembly language program corresponding to the C program shown in the comments:

```
                                     r0703.a
 1 |                                # #include <stdio.h>
 2 |                                # struct Point
 3 |                                # {
 4 |                                #    int x;
 5 |                                #    int y;
 6 |                                # };
 7 |
 8 | a1:         .zero 20           # int a1[5];
 9 | p1:         .zero 8            # struct Point p1;
10 | #==========================================================
11 | main:       .global main       # int main()
12 |                                # {
13 |             addi sp, sp, -28   #    int a2[5];
14 |                                #    struct Point p2;
15 |
16 |                                #    static int a3[5];
17 |                                #    static struct Point p3;
18 |
19 |             li t0, 1           #    a1[1] = 1;
20 |             sw t0, a1+4
21 |             sw t0, p1+4        #    p1.y = 1;
22 |
23 |             sw t0, 12(sp)      #    a2[1] = 1;
24 |             sw t0, 4(sp)       #    p2.y = 1;
25 |
26 |             sw t0, @1a3+4      #    a3[1] = 1;
27 |             sw t0, @2p3+4      #    p3.y = 1;
28 |
29 |             s                  #    debugger inst to display stack
30 |
31 |             li a0, 0           #    return 0;
32 |             jalr x0, 0(ra)
33 |                                # }
34 | @1a3:       .zero 20
35 | @2p3:       .zero 8
```

The global variables a1 and p1 are created with .zero directives on lines 8 and 9. Similarly, the static local variables a3 and p3 are created with .zero directives on lines 34 and 35. The dynamic local variables a2 and p2, on the other hand, are created on the stack by the addi instruction of line13. The array a2 and the struct p2 together require 7 words, which is 28 bytes. Thus, to create a2 and p2 on the stack, the addi instruction on line 13 decrements the sp register by 28.

The five slots of the global a1 array are mapped to memory in the order of increasing index. That is, a1[1] is above a1[0] in memory, a1[2] is above a1[1] in memory, and so on. Thus, the dynamic local array a2 should be mapped to memory in the same way. That is, the lowest word in memory of the stack space allocated for a2 should be mapped to a2[0]. Above that should be the location of a2[1], and so on. Similarly, the dynamic local struct p2 should be mapped to memory that same way the global struct p1 is mapped. p1.y is above p1.x in memory. Thus, p2.y should be above p2.x in memory. With this mapping, we get the following layout of the dynamic local variables on the stack:

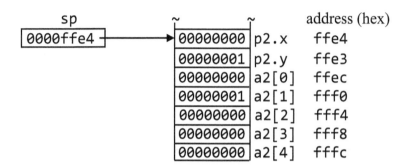

The offset of a2[1] from the location sp points to is 12 bytes. Thus, the instruction that initializes a2[1] to 1 specifies the offset 12 (line 23 in r0703.a). The offset of p2.y from the location sp points to is 4. Thus, the instruction that initializes p2.y to 1 specifies the offset 4 (line 24).

Because all the array indices in r0703.a are constants, the compiler at compile time can determine the appropriate address to access the corresponding array slots. However, if an index is a variable, the address of the corresponding slot has to be determined *at run time*. For example, suppose x is an int variable that contains some index into the a1 array. Then the code for the statement

```
    a1[x] = 5;
```
is
```
        la t0, a1        # get address of a1
        lw t1, x         # get index
        sll t1, t1, 2    # convert index to byte index by multiplying by 4
        add t0, t0, t1   # get address of a[x]
        li t1, 5         # get value to assign
        sw t1, 0(t0)     # store 5 into a[x]
```

Note that the code does not test if the index is in the range 0 to 4 (to ensure that it is within the bounds of the a1 array). This is not an oversight on our part. C compilers do *not* generate code to test the validity of array indices. Thus, if x has an invalid index, the store of 5 will be in some location outside the a1 array. If you want indices to be tested in a C program, you have to write the testing code yourself.

The debugger instruction, s, is on line 29 in r0703.a. If you assemble r0703.a, link with startup code, and run the program, the s instruction will display the dynamic local variables on the stack. You will see on your display

```
Stack:
ffe4: 00000000 ⎫
ffe8: 00000001 ⎬ p2
ffec: 00000000 ⎫
fff0: 00000001 ⎪
fff4: 00000000 ⎬ a2
fff8: 00000000 ⎪
fffc: 00000000 ⎭
```

Compiling Recursive Functions

A *recursive function* is a function that calls itself. For example, in the following program, `fact` is a recursive function. The recursive call is on line 6.

r0704.c

```
 1 #include <stdio.h>
 2 int fact(int n)
 3 {
 4     if (n < 2)
 5         return 1;
 6     return n*fact(n-1);
 7 }
 8 //====================
 9 int main()
10 {
11     int answer;
12     answer = fact(3);
13     printf("%d\n", answer);
14     return 0;
15 }
```

fact calls itself

The `fact` function computes and returns to its caller n factorial, where n is the argument `fact` is passed by the caller. The call of `fact` on line 12 passes 3 to `fact`. Thus, `fact` computes 3 factorial, which is the product of the integers from 3 down to 1 ($3\times2\times1 = 6$). Line 13 then displays the value of 3 factorial returned to `main` by `fact`.

On the first call of `fact`, n has the value of 3. The argument in the recursive call on line 6 is n-1. Thus, on the second call, the parameter n is 2. On the next call, it is 1. On the call when n is 1, the recursive call does not occur. Instead, `fact` returns 1 to its caller, one level up. At that level n is 2, where n and the returned value (which is 1) are multiplied. The product (which is $2\times1 = 1$) is returned to the next level up, where it is multiplied by n (which is 3 at that level). The result is $3\times2\times1 = 6$. This result is returned to `main`, where it is displayed.

If the preceding description has your head spinning, it is not unexpected. Recursion is a difficult concept to understand fully. The best way to master recursion is to mentally execute step-by-step the assembly code in `r0704.a` that corresponds to the C program in `r0704.c`. As you do this, keep track of the contents of the stack and the registers with diagrams. If you do this, perhaps several times, how recursion works will become clear. Recursion is easy to understand once you understand it!

Before we examine the assembler code for our recursive program, let's make an important observation about the recursive call in the C program:

```
6     return n*fact(n-1);
```

Before the product of n and `fact(n-1)` can be computed, the call of `fact` has to be completed. Thus, the argument n (which is in a0) is used *after* the call of `fact`. Recall that a0 is a caller-saved register. That is, the callee has no obligation to return it unmodified to the caller. Thus, before the recursive call, n in a0 should be saved on the stack then restored after the call so that it can be used in the computation of the product. To make the situation even more complicated, by convention fact returns a value via a0. Thus, on return from fact, a0 has the return value and n is on the stack. The return value in a0 is moved into t0, and then a0 is restored with n from the value of n previously saved on the stack. These two values are multiplied, the product, which goes into a0, is then returned to the next level up.

r0704.a

```
 1              # #include <stdio.h>
 2 fact:       .global fact    # int fact(int n)
 3              addi sp, sp, -8  # {
 4              sw ra, 4(sp)
 5              sw a0, 0(sp)
 6
 7              slti t0, a0, 2   #    if (n < 2)
 8              beq t0, x0, recurse
 9
10              li a0, 1
11              addi sp, sp, 8
12              jalr x0, 0(ra)   #         return 1;
13
14 recurse:    addi a0, a0, -1  #    return n*fact(n-1);
15              jal ra, fact
16              mv t0, a0
17              lw a0, 0(sp)
18              mul a0, a0, t0
19
20              lw ra, 4(sp)
21              addi sp, sp, 8
22              jalr x0, 0(ra)
23                              # }
24 #===================================================
25 main:       .global main    # int main()
26              addi sp, sp, -8  # {
27              sw ra, 4(sp)
28              sw s0, 0(sp)     #    int answer;
29
30              li a0, 3         #    answer = fact(3);
31              jal ra, fact
32
33              mv s0, a0        #    answer = fact(3);
34
35              dout s0          #    printf("%d\n", answer);
36              nl
37
38              li a0, 0         #    return 0;
39              lw s0, 0(sp)
40              lw ra, 4(sp)
41              addi sp, sp, 8
42              jalr x0, 0(ra)
43                              # }
```

Let's look at the code that does all this.

On entry into `fact`, line 5 saves the value in `a0` (which is n) on the stack:

```
5                  sw a0, 0(sp)
```

The sequence for the recursive call firsts computes the value of the argument `n-1` by decrementing the value in `a0` and then calls `fact`:

```
14 recurse:    addi a0, a0, -1        #     return n*fact(n-1);
15             jal ra, fact
```

On return from `fact`, the return value in `a0` is moved into `t0`:

```
16             mv t0, a0
```

Next, `a0` is restored with the saved value of n:

```
17             lw a0, 0(sp)
```

n in `a0` and the returned value in `t0` are then multiplied:

```
18             mul a0, a0, t0
```

Finally, the returning sequence is executed with the new return value in `a0`:

```
20             lw ra, 4(sp)
21             addi sp, sp, 8
22             jalr x0, 0(ra)
```

On entry into `fact`, two words are reserved in which the return address and n (in `a0`) are saved. On exit, `ra` is restored with the return address, and the two words previously reserved on the stack are popped (by adding 8 to `sp`). `a0` holds the return value (the product `n*fact(n-1)`). Thus, `a0` should *not* be restored with the value of n that was saved on the stack.

A great tool for investigating how recursion works is the debugger in the `rv` program. For example, suppose you assemble `r0704.a` by entering

```
rv r0704.a
```

then link with startup code by entering

Link `r0704.o` first

```
rv r0704.o su.o
```

and then execute the executable file `link.e` produced by the linker by entering

Activate the debugger

```
rv link.e -d
```

The `-d` command line argument activates the debugger. Then enter b0

which sets a break point at location 0. Because r0704.o was linked first, location 0 is the starting location in memory of the machine code for the fact function. Then each time you enter g, execution proceeds at full speed until the breakpoint is reached, at which point execution is paused and the debugger is activated. Thus, the debugger is activated each time the fact function starts executing. During each pause, you can use the m command to display memory, the x command to display registers, or the s command to display the stack. Using these debugger commands, you can see how the registers change and how the stack grows as the recursion proceeds.

An even easier way of observing what is going on as the recursion proceeds is to insert the s debugger instruction on line 6 in r0704.a. This instruction displays the stack. Thus, without any breakpoints, each time fact is entered, the stack is displayed right after ra and a0 are saved on the stack (you can also insert the x and m debugger instructions to see the registers and memory). Here is the display that you will see with the s instruction inserted:

```
Stack:
fff0:  00000003   (n on the first call of fact)
fff4:  00000058   (main address fact returns to)
fff8:  00000000   (saved s0)
fffc:  000000c0   (startup code address main returns to)

Stack:
ffe8:  00000002   (n on the second call of fact)
ffec:  0000002c   (fact address fact returns to)
fff0:  00000003   (n on the first call of fact)
fff4:  00000058   (main address fact returns to)
fff8:  00000000   (saved s0)
fffc:  000000c0   (startup code address main returns to)

Stack:
ffe0:  00000001   (n on the third call of fact)
ffe4:  0000002c   (fact address fact returns to)
ffe8:  00000002   (n on the second call of fact)        Stack frames created by fact
ffec:  0000002c   (fact address fact returns to)
fff0:  00000003   (n on the first call of fact)
fff4:  00000058   (main address fact returns to)
fff8:  00000000   (saved s0)                            Stack frame created by main
fffc:  000000c0   (startup code address main returns to)
6                 (output, 6 factorial)
```

You can see that each time fact is called the stack grows by two words—the return address and the value in a0 (which is n)—in the downward direction. We refer to these two words as the *stack frame* for that call. Each call produces its own stack frame. On each call, sp points to the stack frame for that call. For example, on the third call of fact, sp contains the address ffe0. Thus, it is pointing to the lower word in the third call's stack frame. Similarly, on the second call of fact, sp is pointing to the lower word in that call's stack frame. sp provides the base address of the current stack frame which the called function uses to access its stack frame.

Let's summarize what a function should do on entry and exit, and before and after calling another function. Suppose f is a function that calls the function g, where g is a *leaf function*. That is, g does not call any functions.

- Everything on the stack associated with the call of f is referred to as the *stack frame* or *activation record* for that call. On entry, f should immediately reserve space on the stack for its *entire* stack frame, generally with a single addi instruction unless the frame size is larger than 2048 bytes (a single addi instruction can decrement the sp register by at most 2048). Creating the entire stack frame on entry into f has two advantages: 1) It is more efficient than creating it incrementally (because each increment requires an addi instruction to decrement the sp register). 2) The offsets to the items on the stack do not change during the execution of the function because the address in sp does not change.
- If f needs any of the values in the "a" registers that are passed to it after the call of g, then on entry f should save them on the stack, and then restore them after the call of g.
- Because f calls a function, on entry f should save the ra register on the stack.
- If f modifies any callee-saved registers (an "s" register), on entry f should save them on the stack and restore them on exit.
- On entry, f should allocate on the stack any of its dynamic local variables not mapped to registers.
- If f loads a caller-saved register with value before the call of g that it needs after the call, f should save the register on the stack before the call and restore it after the call. Note that f should *not* save the register on entry—because it has not yet loaded it with a value. Instead, it should save the register only after it loads it with the value that it will subsequently need.
- Before returning to its caller, f should restore the ra register and all the callee-saved registers it previously saved, then pop its entire stack frame, generally with a single addi instruction that adds the stack frame size to the sp register. This restores the sp register to the value it had when f was called.
- g follows the same protocol as f except it does not save the ra register (because g is not a caller).
- If the caller of f has to pass f more than eight arguments, the caller of f passes the first eight in a0 though a7. It passes the arguments after the eighth via the stack. Specifically, the caller of f pushes the arguments after the eighth onto the stack before it calls f. On return, the caller of f pops these arguments off the stack.

Here is a picture of the stack when f is executing, assuming the caller of f passed f nine arguments, and f has a value in t0 that it will need after the call of g:

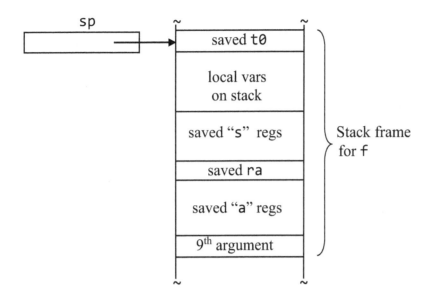

Problems

1) Should a function always save `ra` on entry and restore it on exit?

2) Under what circumstances should a caller save a caller-saved register it uses?

3) If A calls B, and B calls C, and C modifies `s0`, but B does not use `s0`, is it still necessary for C to save and then restore `s0`?

4) If a C program has only one static local variable, may the label on its `.word` directive be simply the C-level name of the variable?

5) What problem might result if the slots of a dynamic local array are mapped differently to memory than the slots of a global array.

6) Write a C program that includes a *recursive* function named `countdown`. Your `main` function should read in a positive number n and pass it to `countdown`. `countdown` should display the integers from n down to 0. Translate to assembly language, assemble, link with startup code, and run.

7) Write a C program that includes a recursive function `fib` that computes and returns the nth Fibonacci number ($fib_1 = 1$, $fib_2 = 1$, $fib_n = f_{n-1} + fib_{n-2}$ for $n > 2$). Translate your C code to assembly language. Assemble, link with startup code, and run with `rv`. Use your program to determine the 12th Fibonacci number. Is your recursive function an efficient way to compute Fibonacci numbers?

8) Same as preceding problem but use a loop instead of recursion.

Translate the following programs to assembly language, assemble, link with startup code, and run. Comment your assembly code with the corresponding C statements. The output of your assembly language programs should be identical to the output of the corresponding C programs.

```
9) // rx0709.c =====================
#include <stdio.h>
void g()
{
    printf("in g\n");
}
void f(void)
{
    g();
}
int main()
{
    f();
    return 0;
}
```

```
10)// rx0710.c =====================
#include <stdio.h>
void g(int v1, int v2, int v3, int v4, int v5, int v6, int v7, int v8,
        int v9, int v10)
{
    printf("%d\n", v1+v2+v3+v4+v5+v6+v7+v8+v9+v10);
}
void f(void)
{
    g(1, 2, 3, 4, 5, 6, 7, 8, 9, 10);
    printf("down\n");
}
int main()
{
    printf("hello\n");
    f();
    printf("goodbye\n");
    return 0;
}
```

```
11)// rx0711.c =====================
#include <stdio.h>
int a = 5;
void f(int *x)
{
    *x = *x + 1;
}
```

```
int main()
{
    f(&a);
    printf("%d\n", a);
    return 0;
}
```

12)// rx0712.c ====================
```
#include <stdio.h>
void f(int x)
{
if (x > 0)
    {
        printf("%d\n", x);
        f(x-1);
        printf("%d\n", x);
    }
}
int main()
{
    f(3);
    return 0;
}
```

13)// rx0713.c ===================
```
#include <stdio.h>
void g(int x, int y)
{
    printf("%d %d\n", x, y);
}
void f(int x, int y)
{
    g(y, x);
}
int main()
{
    f(3, 4);
    return 0;
}
```

14)// rx0714.c ===================
```
#include <stdio.h>
void f(int x, int a[])
{
    printf("%d\n", a[x]);
}
int main()
{
```

```
    int a[10], i = 6;
    a[1] = 7;
    a[i] = 11;
    f(1, a);
    f(6, a);
    return 0;
}
```

15) // rx0715.c ====================
```
#include <stdio.h>
void f()
{
    static int x = 3;
    printf("%d\n", x);
    x = x + 1;
}
int main()
{
    f();
    f();
    return 0;
}
```

16) // rx0716.c ====================
```
    #include <stdio.h>
    void f()
    {
        static int x = 3;
        printf("%d\n", x);
        x = x + 1;
    }
    void g()
    {
        static int x = 5;
        printf("%d\n", x);
        x = x+ 1;
    }
    int main()
    {
        f();
        f();
        g();
        g();
        return 0;
    }
```

17) // rx0717.c ====================
```
    #include <stdio.h>
```

```
    int a = 7;
    int f(int *x, int y)
    {
        int sum;
        printf("%d\n", *x);
        sum = *x + y;
        return sum;
    }
    int main()
    {
        int ans;
        ans = f(&a, 11);
        printf("ans = %d\n", ans);
        return 0;
    }
```

18) `// rx0718.c ====================`

```
    #include <stdio.h>
    int x = 2;
    void f(int *p)
    {
        x = x + 5;
        *p = *p + 10;
        printf("%d %d\n", x, *p);
    }
    int main()
    {
        static int x = 3;
        f(&x);
        printf("%d\n", x);
        return 0;
    }
```

19) `// rx0719.c ====================`

```
    #include <stdio.h>
    struct X
    {
        int m, n;
    };
    int x, y, z = 6;
    void f(int *a, int b, int c, struct X *p)
    {
        static int h, i, j;
        b = c = h = i = ++j;
        printf("%d %d\n", *a, b);
        (*p).m = b;
        (*p).n = c;
    }
```

```
    int main()
    {
        struct X s;
        x = 1;
        y = 2;
        f(&x, y, z, &s);
        printf("%d %d\n", s.m, s.n);
        f(&z, y, z, &s);
        printf("%d %d\n", s.m, s.n);
        return 0;
    }


20) // rx0720.c ====================
#include <stdio.h>
int f(int a, int b)
{
    if (b == 0)
        return 0;
    return f(a, b-1) + a;
}
int main()
{
    printf("%d\n", f(2, 3));
    return 0;
}
```

Appendix A: ASCII

Hex	Decimal		Hex	Decimal		Hex	Decimal	
20	32	\<blank>	40	64	@	60	96	`
21	33	!	41	65	A	61	97	a
22	34	"	42	66	B	62	98	b
23	35	#	43	67	C	63	99	c
24	36	$	44	68	D	64	100	d
25	37	%	45	69	E	65	101	e
26	38	&	46	70	F	66	102	f
27	38	'	47	71	G	67	103	g
28	40	(	48	72	H	69	104	h
29	41	)	49	73	I	69	105	i
2A	42	*	4A	74	J	6A	106	j
2B	43	+	4B	75	K	6B	107	k
2C	44	,	4C	76	L	6C	108	l
2D	45	-	4D	77	M	6D	109	m
2E	46	.	4E	78	N	6E	110	n
2F	47	/	4F	79	O	6F	111	o
30	48	0	50	80	P	70	112	p
31	49	1	51	81	Q	71	113	q
32	50	2	52	82	R	72	114	r
33	51	3	53	83	S	73	114	s
34	52	4	54	84	T	74	116	t
35	53	5	55	85	U	75	117	u
36	54	6	56	86	V	76	118	v
37	55	7	57	87	W	77	119	w
38	56	8	58	88	X	78	120	x
39	57	9	59	89	Y	79	121	y
3A	58	:	5A	90	Z	7A	122	z
3B	59	;	5B	91	[	7B	123	{
3C	60	<	5C	92	\	7C	124	|
3D	61	=	5D	93	]	7D	125	}
3E	62	>	5E	94	^	7E	126	~
3F	63	?	5F	95	_			

Important Control Characters

Hex	Decimal		Meaning
09	9	\t	Horizontal tab
0A	10	\n	Line feed (i.e., newline)
0D	13	\r	Carriage return

Appendix B: RISC-V Summary

Register name	Alias	Use	Saver
x0	zero	read-only (0)	n/a
x1	ra	return address	caller
x2	sp	stack pointer	callee
x3	gp	global pointer	n/a
x4	tp	thread pointer	n/a
x5-x7	t0-t2	temporary	caller
x8-x9	s0-s1	saved	callee
x10-x11	a0-a1	arguments/return values	caller
x12-x17	a2-a7	arguments	caller
x18-x27	s2-s11	saved	callee
x28-x31	t3-t6	temporary	caller

31 25	24 20	19 15	14 12	11 7	6 0	
funct7	rs2	rs1	funct3	rd	opcode	R-type
imm[11:0]		rs1	000	rd	opcode	I-type
imm[11:5]	rs2	rs1	funct3	imm[4:0]	opcode	S-type
imm[12|10:5]	rs2	rs1	funct3	imm[4:1|11]	opcode	B-type
imm[31:12]				rd	opcode	U-type
imm[20|10:1|11|19:12]				rd	opcode	J-type

Pseudoinstructions

bgt *rs1, rs2, label*   j *label*   seqz *rd, rs1*

ble *rs1, rs2, label*   jal *label*   snez *rd, rs1*

bgtu *rs1, rs2, label*   jr *rs1*   sltz *rd, rs1*

bleu *rs1, rs2, label*   jalr *rs1*   sgtz *rd, rs1*

                        ret

beqz *rs1, label*   li *rd, constant*

bnez *rs1, label*   la *rd, label*

bltz *rs1 label*   mv *rd, rs1*

bgez *rs1, label*   not *rd, rs1*

blez *rs1, label*   neg rd, rs1

Directives

.ascii   .globl

.asciz   .rodata

.bss   .space

.data   .start

.dword   .string

.equ   .text

.extern   .word

.global   .zero

RV32M Standard Extension

31 25	24 20	19 15	14 12	11 7	6 0	
0000001	rs2	rs1	000	rd	0110011	mul
0000001	rs2	rs1	001	rd	0110011	mulh
0000001	rs2	rs1	010	rd	0110011	mulhsu
0000001	rs2	rs1	011	rd	0110011	mulhu
0000001	rs2	rs1	100	rd	0110011	div
0000001	rs2	rs1	101	rd	0110011	divu
0000001	rs2	rs1	110	rd	0110011	rem
0000001	rs2	rs1	111	rd	0110011	remu

RV32I Base Instruction Set[1]

31 25	24 20	19 15	14 12	11 7	6 0	
imm[31:12]				rd	0110111	lui
imm[31:12]				rd	0010111	auipc
imm[20|10:1|11|19:12]				rd	1101111	jal
imm[11:0]		rs1	000	rd	1100111	jalr
imm[12|10:5]	rs2	rs1	000	imm[4:1|11]	1100011	beq
imm[12|10:5]	rs2	rs1	001	imm[4:1|11]	1100011	bne
imm[12|10:5]	rs2	rs1	100	imm[4:1|11]	1100011	blt
imm[12|10:5]	rs2	rs1	101	imm[4:1|11]	1100011	bge
imm[12|10:5]	rs2	rs1	110	imm[4:1|11]	1100011	bltu
imm[12|10:5]	rs2	rs1	111	imm[4:1|11]	1100011	bgeu
imm[11:0]		rs1	000	rd	0000011	lb
imm[11:0]		rs1	001	rd	0000011	lh
imm[11:0]		rs1	010	rd	0000011	lw
imm[11:0]		rs1	100	rd	0000011	lbu
imm[11:0]		rs1	101	rd	0000011	lhu
imm[11:5]	rs2	rs1	000	imm[4:0]	0100011	sb
imm[11:5]	rs2	rs1	001	imm[4:0]	0100011	sh
imm[11:5]	rs2	rs1	010	imm[4:0]	0100011	sw
imm[11:0]		rs1	000	rd	0010011	addi
imm[11:0]		rs1	010	rd	0010011	slti
imm[11:0]		rs1	011	rd	0010011	sltiu
imm[11:0]		rs1	100	rd	0010011	xori
imm[11:0]		rs1	110	rd	0010011	ori
imm[11:0]		rs1	111	rd	0010011	andi
0000000	shamt	rs1	001	rd	0010011	slli
0000000	shamt	rs1	101	rd	0010011	srli
0100000	shamt	rs1	101	rd	0010011	srai
0000000	rs2	rs1	000	rd	0110011	add
0100000	rs2	rs1	000	rd	0110011	sub
0000000	rs2	rs1	001	rd	0110011	sll
0000000	rs2	rs1	010	rd	0110011	slt
0000000	rs2	rs1	011	rd	0110011	sltu
0000000	rs2	rs1	100	rd	0110011	xor
0000000	rs2	rs1	101	rd	0110011	srl
0100000	rs2	rs1	101	rd	0110011	sra
0000000	rs2	rs1	110	rd	0110011	or
0000000	rs2	rs1	111	rd	0110011	and
0000000			000		0000000	halt[2]
0000001			000		0000000	nl[2]
0000010		rs1	000		0000000	dout[2]
0000011		rs1	000		0000000	udout[2]
0000100		rs1	000		0000000	hout[2]
0000101		rs1	000		0000000	aout[2]
0000110		rs1	000		0000000	sout[2]
0000111			000	rd	0000000	din[2]
0001000			000	rd	0000000	hin[2]
0001001			000	rd	0000000	ain[2]
0001010		rs1	000		0000000	sin[2]
0001011			000		0000000	m[2]
0001100			000		0000000	x[2]
0001101			000		0000000	s[2]
0001110			000		0000000	bp[2]
0001111		rs1	000		0000000	ddout[2]
0010000		rs1	000		0000000	dudout[2]
0010001		rs1	000		0000000	dhout[2]

1: `fence`, `fence.1`, `ecall`, `ebreak` not supported by `rv`   2: rv-supported—not in RISC-V

Appendix C: References

1. `risv.org`
   Website for the RISC-V Foundation.

2. Search for "mit risc-v" on YouTube.
   Excellent online course on RISC-V from MIT.

3. *Computer Organization and Design RISC-V Edition: The Hardware Software Interface*
   David A. Patterson, John L. Hennessey
   Morgan Kaufman, 2017
   An excellent introduction to RISC-V in the context of the premier computer organization textbook.

4. *The RISC-V Reader: An Open Architecture*
   David A. Patterson, Andrew Waterman
   Strawberry Canyon, 2017
   The definitive reference on RISC-V.

5. *Constructing a Microprogrammed Computer*
   Anthony J. Dos Reis
   KDP (amazon), 2019
   Shows how to implement a variety of instruction sets via microprogramming.

6. *Writing Interpreters and Compilers for the Raspberry Pi Using Python, 2018*
   Anthony J. Dos Reis
   KDP (amazon), 2018
   A readable introduction to compiler and interpreter construction.

7. *C and C++ Under the Hood*
   Anthony J. Dos Reis
   KDP (amazon), 2019
   An extensive examination of C and C++ at the assembly language level.

8. *Raspberry Pi Assembly Language*
   Bruce Smith
   BSB, 2016
   An introduction to Raspberry Pi Assembly Language Programming.

9. *Assembly Language Step by Step*
   Jeff Duntermann
   Wiley, 2009
   Assembly language programming in the Linux environment.

Index